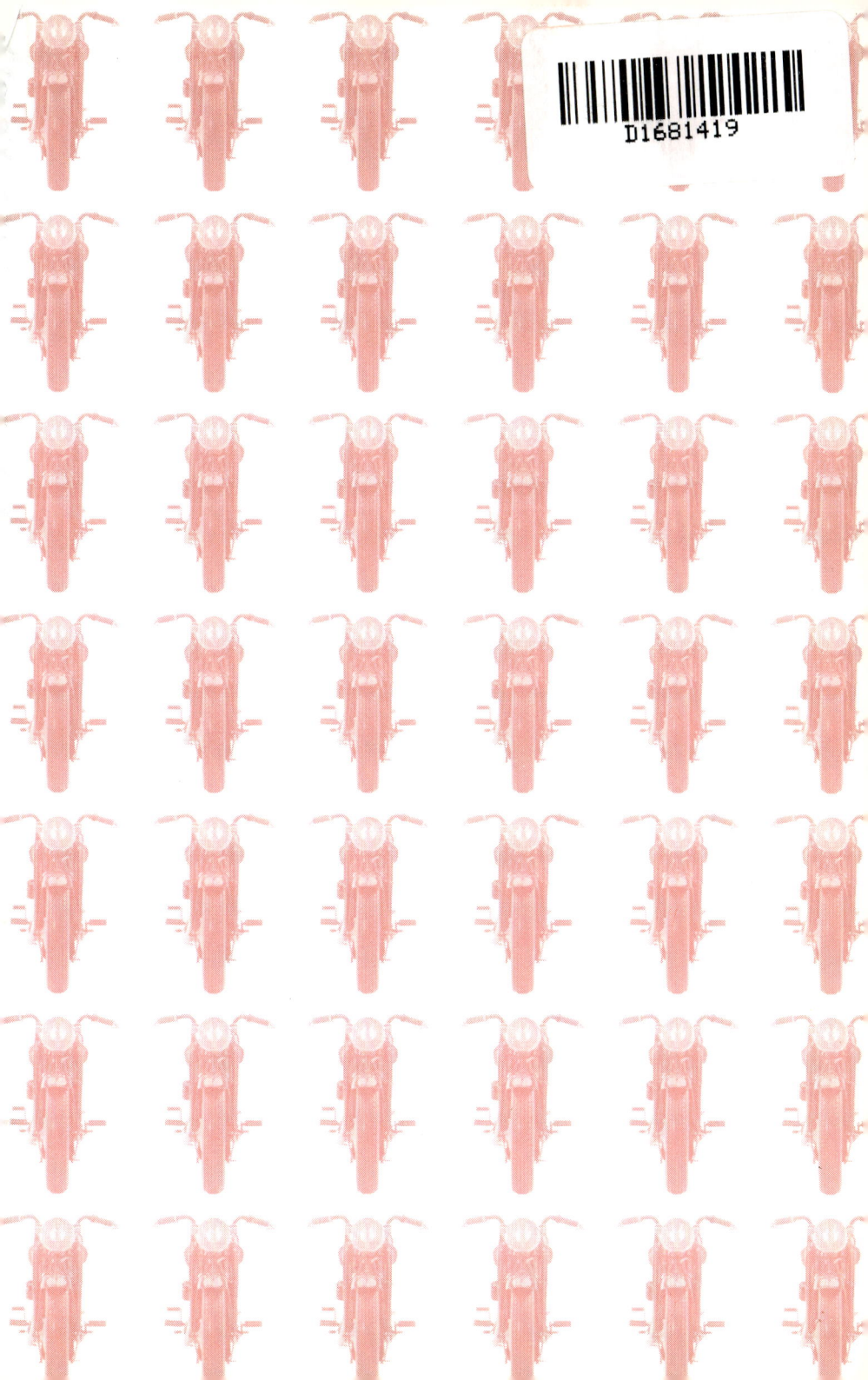

MOTORCYCLES

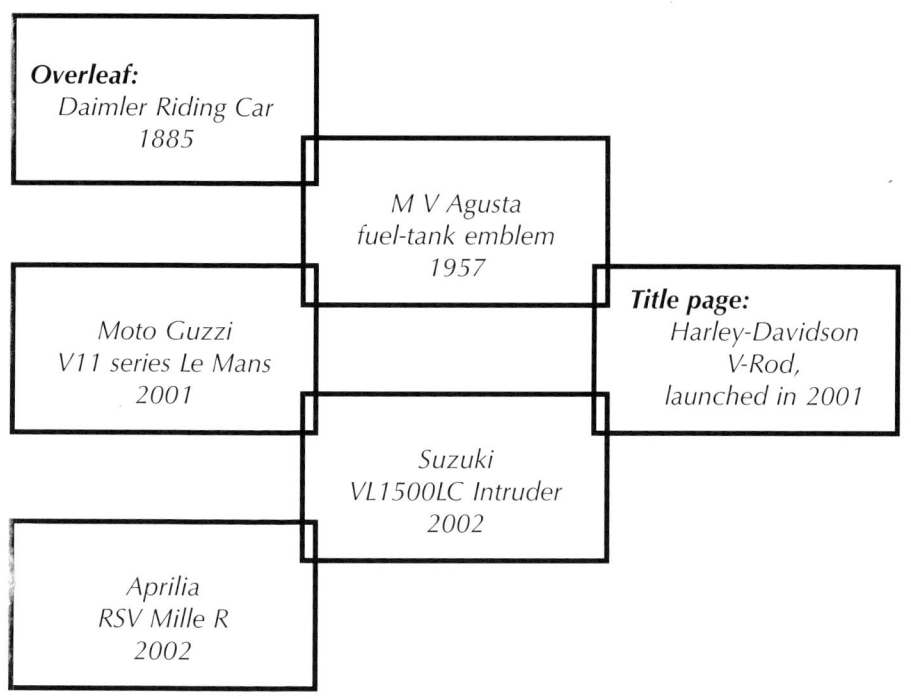

Overleaf:
Daimler Riding Car
1885

M V Agusta
fuel-tank emblem
1957

Moto Guzzi
V11 series Le Mans
2001

Title page:
Harley-Davidson
V-Rod,
launched in 2001

Suzuki
VL1500LC Intruder
2002

Aprilia
RSV Mille R
2002

MOTORCYCLES

Caxton Editions

First published in Great Britain by
Caxton Editions
20 Bloomsbury Street
London WC1B 3JH

This edition copyright
© 2003 Caxton Publishing Group

Unless otherwise credited, all of the photographs
in this publication appear by kind permission of the manufacturers, through
the courtesy of Aldino™
These pages: *a 2002 Lightning X1 followed by a Firebolt XB9R, both products
of the highly individual American Buell company*

Derek Avery has asserted his right to be
regarded as the author of this work
in accordance with the
Copyright, Designs and Patents Act 1988

All rights reserved. No part of this publication
may be reproduced, stored in a retrieval system,
or transmitted in any form or by any means,
electronic, mechanical, photocopying, recording
or otherwise, without the prior permission in writing
of the copyright holders.

ISBN 1 84067 320 6

Designed and produced by
Superlaunch Limited
PO Box 207
Abingdon
Oxfordshire OX13 6TA

Imagesetting by International Graphic Services, Bath
Printed and bound in Singapore

CONTENTS

FOREWORD 6
EVOLUTION AND HISTORY 8
A CENTURY OF MOTORCYCLES 32
MOTORCYCLE ANATOMY 78
MODERN MOTORCYCLES 82
GLOSSARY 150
INDEX 156

FOREWORD

The marriage of a pair of wheels and an internal combustion engine represents a perfect union, and throughout the last century people built, tinkered and relentlessly developed the combination to improve its overall harmony.

    Beginning with Daimler's 1885 Riding Car, built of wood, brass and steel, to today's sophisticated harnessing of power and efficiency, the motorcycle represents more than just a form of transport.
    Coupled with an extraordinary fascination for the beautiful machine, which goes far beyond the mere metal from which it is built, different people want different machines for different reasons and for a wide variety of uses, but above all else, the appeal of the motorcycle can always be expressed as the equation of 2 wheels + 1 engine = fun.

Above: the 2002 Triumph Daytona 955i

Below: *the 1885 Daimler Riding Car*

EVOLUTION AND HISTORY

The first-ever motorcycle in the world, the Daimler Riding Car, took to the streets of Bad Cannstatt, near Stuttgart, Germany, on 10 November 1885. It was the result of experiments by the two inseparable inventors, the engineer Gottlieb Daimler (1834–1900) and the draughtsman Wilhelm Maybach (1846–1929).

EVOLUTION AND HISTORY

EVOLUTION AND HISTORY

The main picture shows the world's first motorcycle in the workshop in which it was created; the Daimler Riding Car in the converted greenhouse at Bad Cannstatt. **Inset,** *a portrait of Gottlieb Daimler*

> ## EINSPUR: 1885
>
> ## Specification
>
> **Country of origin:** Germany
> **Engine:** single-cylinder
> **Capacity:** 264cc
> **Output:** 5hp
> **Bore and stroke:** 58 x 100mm (2.28 x 3.94in)
> **Dimensions:** weight 90kg (198lb)
> **Performance:** top speed 12km/h (7.45mph)

Born the son of a master baker, Daimler had first became an apprentice gunsmith before joining Reutlingen Brotherhood as technical manager. It was here that he was to meet Maybach. Daimler established his own business in 1882, and was joined by Maybach in offices in a converted greenhouse in the park behind the Daimler villa, which today is maintained as a museum.

Daimler had been working on the development of a small light engine that would be suitable for universal application. On 3 April 1885 he took out patent DRP 34926, for an engine that had an enclosed crankcase and a single vertical cylinder, and which later became known as the grandfather clock. Later in the same year, this 265cc 0.5-horsepower internal combustion engine was fitted into a wooden-framed two-wheeler. This *Einspur* 'one track', known to us as the Daimler Riding Car, was ridden through the streets of Stuttgart by Daimler's son, Paul, on the first-ever motorcycle ride.

The first production motorcycle, *illustrated right*, appeared in 1894. It was produced by Hildebrand & Wolfmüller, the German company of Heinrich and Wilhelm Hildebrand and Alois Wolfmüller. It was powered by an extremely large water-cooled, four-stroke petrol engine, which was positioned where the pedals are on a modern pushbike. It had a steel frame, as well as John Boyd Dunlop's (1840–1921) recently-invented pneumatic tyres.

At about the same time, after several attempts to develop a viable steam-powered bike had failed, a pair of French pioneers, Comte Albert de Dion (1856–1946) and his partner Georges Bouton (1847–1938), eventually turned to the internal combustion engine and produced a single-cylinder, four-stroke petrol engine of about 125cc, which they mounted in a tricycle. Their engine had approximately twice the power of Daimler's, was also rated at 0.5hp, and

EVOLUTION AND HISTORY

Hildebrand & Wolfmüller: 1894

Specification

Country of origin: Germany
Engine: two-cylinder, four-stroke
Capacity: 1,488cc
Output: 2.5hp at 240rpm
Bore and stroke: 90 x 117mm (3.54 x 4.61in)
Dimensions: weight 90kg (198lb)
Performance: top speed 40km/h (24.84mph)

revved at 1,800rpm. Unfortunately for the French inventors, their engine was copied by numerous motorcycle firms as production spread across Europe, but by the end of the nineteenth century the firm of De Dion, Bouton et Cie had embarked on producing engines which were for sale over the counter. They also licensed production in England, Germany, Belgium and the United States.

The variety of early designs and the siting of the engine was manifold, with some engines being mounted above or at the side of the front wheel; others

EVOLUTION AND HISTORY

were mounted above or behind the rear wheel, while the problem of connecting one of the wheels to the continuous drive belt proved to be a major stumbling block for many would-be manufacturers.

The definitive solution was first put into effect by two enthusiastic Russian exiles living in Paris, Michel and Eugene Werner. In 1901, after much experimentation, they produced a bike, *illustrated above*, that set the pattern for the twentieth century. Their patented New Werner layout placed the 2hp 230cc engine low down in a diamond-shaped steel frame midway between the two road wheels, just in front of the pedalling gear behind the front down-tube.

The design also featured a leather belt to drive the rear wheel, a bicycle-style saddle and wheel-rim brakes. The overall effect provided considerably improved stability for the motorcycle, from a much lower centre of gravity.

At the beginning of the twentieth century motorcycle production was being pioneered in continental Europe, where a growing enthusiasm and roads that were generally free of speed restrictions combined to fuel the quest for speed, which in turn placed increased demands on bike technology.

The spark plug was invented in 1902, and in the following year the German engineer, Robert Bosch, invented the high-tension magneto system which was designed to produce a controlled spark to ignite the vapours in the combustion chamber at exactly the right time. This combination of spark plug and magneto was quickly adopted by the major manufacturers, and has remained the basis of all car and motorcycle ignition systems to this day.

EVOLUTION AND HISTORY

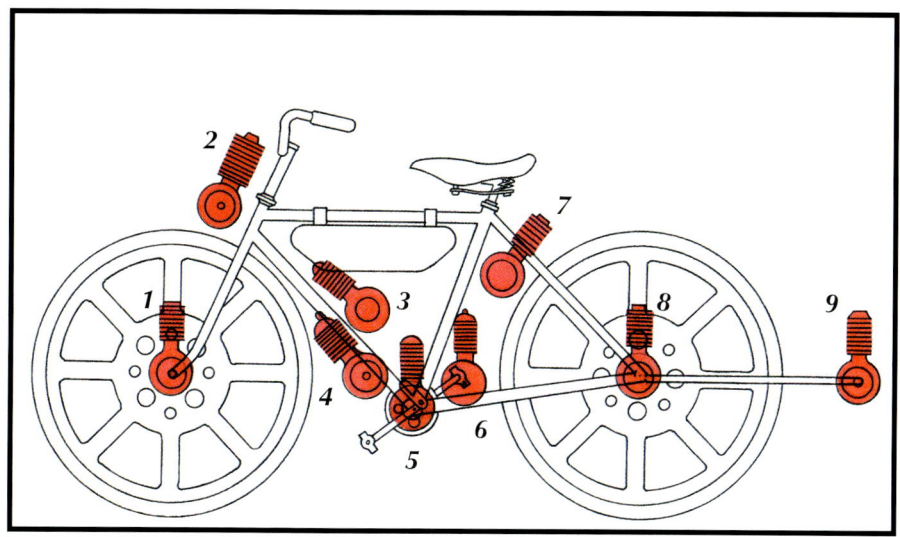

Above: a few of the initial attempts to site the engine, a dilemma for all the early manufacturers

Key
1 Singer
2 Werner
3 Powerful
4 Triumph
5 Hildebrand & Wolfm ller
6 Beeston
7 Ormonde
8 Singer
9 Humber

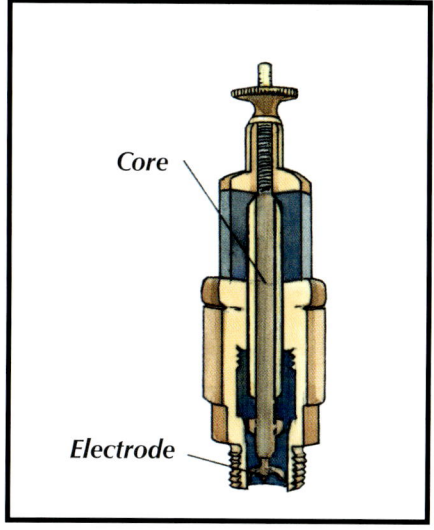

Right: an early spark plug, revealing the core and central electrode

Further rapid development led to improved suspension: the front-end parallel-slider fork that had compression springs in the shafts was developed by Alfred Drew in 1906, and greatly improved the handling and the steering properties of the racing bike in addition to providing greater comfort.

EVOLUTION AND HISTORY

Left: *a 1902 Indian brochure;* **above,** *the 1908 Diamond-Framed Racer was its first-ever racer to be made*

The next major improvement was to the gearing, and this came by courtesy of the engineer Oscar Handstrom and the racer George Hendee, who together had founded the Indian Motorcycle Company of Springfield, Massachusetts, in 1901. They wanted to replace the belt system, and had been experimenting with a two-speed centre shaft transmission that incorporated a clutch, which they finally succeeded in integrating with a drive chain and rear-wheel gear sprockets. In 1911 Indian V-twin four-stroke motorcycles with the new gearing took the first three places in the Manx Tourist Trophy race, assuring the success of the new system.

Such companies as Indian, Harley-Davidson and Henderson thrived during the pioneering years of motorcycling in the United States, to the extent that in 1913, the year in which it introduced rear suspension, Indian produced a total of 31,950 cycles, and also had 42 per cent of the American market. By 1914 it boasted the largest motorcycle factory in the world, with 3,000 employees and a 11.27km (7-mile) assembly line in a 93,000m^2 (1 million sq ft) factory, which was colloquially known as the wigwam.

Harley-Davidson, which was Indian's largest rival along with ACE, Excelsior and Pierce, did not drop its belt drive until 1914; but a year later it had introduced the first three-speed transmission. The hotbed of motorcycle invention by then

EVOLUTION AND HISTORY

Right: a 1914 Peugeot brochure, and *below,* its 345cc Paris-Nice 1914 model had a top speed of 70km/h (43mph)

17

was well and truly in America, where the twist-grip throttle control, the drum brake on the rear wheel, the foot-operated clutch, and the starter motor were all developed at about the same time.

Elsewhere the British-built Scott had featured a water-cooled two-stroke engine, the world's first kick-start and telescopic front forks by 1910, and by the time of the outbreak of the First World War the French Peugeot had a vertical-twin race bike with twin cams and four-valve cylinder heads.

The effect of the war combined with competitively-priced motorcars such as the Model T Ford to drive many manufacturers into bankruptcy, in both Europe and North America. However, although the mass-produced motorcar had taken over in North America, by the end of the 1920s European bike manufacture was booming again with companies such as Benelli, BMW, Matchless, Moto Guzzi, Triumph, Velocette and Zündapp (Zünderland Apparatebau GmbH) producing a variety of very noteworthy bikes that were capable of exceeding speeds of 160km/h (100mph) on the board racing tracks. European companies such as BMW with its horizontally-opposed twin-cylinder four-strokes, and Moto Guzzi with its lightweight ohc four-strokes, had both made their trail-blazing appearances

Below: *between 1923 and 1926 a total of 3,100 horizontally-opposed R 32 motorcycles were produced at the BMW works in Munich, Germany*

EVOLUTION AND HISTORY

Above: *a restored 1926 James 498cc ohv Sports V-Twin*

by the mid-1920s, and benefitted from the demands of war. These had resulted in the production of harder steels and lighter and stronger alloys, which helped to produce a more durable engine capable of greater output and improved performance. Side valves had eventually been replaced by push-rod operated overhead valves, which in turn had given way to overhead camshaft (ohc) engines.

By the 1930s all of the components of the modern bike were readily available. The racing engineer Harold Willis had invented the positive-stop foot gear-change mechanism, which provided a tremendous advantage over the slow and laborious hand levers. As far as the engine was concerned, there were the two-strokes with rotary valves which had been pioneered by Scott and Vitesse, three-cylinder double ohc four-strokes pioneered by Motto Guzzi, and the four-strokes with four valves per cylinder that had been introduced by Rudge.

The beleaguered manufacturers continued to press forward in America, with Indian introducing its four-cylinder motor in 1927 and Harley-Davidson its 290cc (17.7cu in) engine the following year. The American manufacturers also introduced front brakes, re-circulating oil systems, the buddy seat and the brake light in the early 1930s.

EVOLUTION AND HISTORY

Above: *a 1934 brochure advertising Ariel's bestselling 596cc ohc Square Four. The 498cc Square Four had been introduced in 1931, with the four air-cooled cylinders set in a square formation and the ohv gear operated by a chain-driven camshaft*

The European motorcycle industry was in a healthy state towards the end of the 1930s; development and competition had led to the introduction by both Norton and BMW of hydraulically-damped telescopic front wheel springs. Reputations for reliability were growing, with the Ariel Square Four 1000cc tourer attaining a pinnacle of sophistication immediately before the Second World War.

The outbreak of the war signalled the end of the road for many of the prestigious names of the previous era. Renowned British companies such as Brough, New Imperial, Rudge and Sunbeam were lost, and though others switched to manufacturing war materials they never returned to motorcycle production.

Across the Atlantic the story was very different, for although the stock market crash of 1929 had seen the utter devastation of the motorcycle industry, the two remaining marques of Indian and Harley-Davidson were approached by the

EVOLUTION AND HISTORY

War Department to build a special military bike. Its requirement was for a rugged 500cc (30 cu in) twin, and whereas Harley had modified its 1928 Forty-five, Indian produced an inadequate, under-powered 500 based on its Junior Scout. The Indian-built machine proved to be of very little practical use, while 88,000 Harley WLAs were produced in dozens of versions and widely used by all of the major Allied Forces, with thousands even being shipped to Russia.

The return to peace saw mixed fortunes for the motorcycle industry, for whereas Indian became defunct along with many of its European brethren, there was also huge success for those such as Agusta, AJS, Norton and NSU. Just as they had forty years earlier, the manufacturers of components such as two-stroke engines and gearboxes were again selling them on to small companies such as DKW (Germany), Francis-Barnett (England) and SM (Poland) which between them produced an army of cheap lightweight tourers.

Below: *a 1944 Harley-Davidson 1,212cc (74 cu in) V-Twin Model U of the U.S. Navy, complete with its Thompson sub-machine gun. Up to ten clips and one drum of .45 calibre ammunition was carried in a storage compartment positioned on the other side of the bike's front tyre. The Harley's top speed was 140km/h (87mph), but all of the American motorcycles built for the Second World War, which were V-twins, out-performed their European contemporaries in road work. The most popular British military motorcycle was the Matchless G3L; other models included the Ariel NH and the Triumph HRW*

EVOLUTION AND HISTORY

Above: *the BMW R 75; a ponderous vehicle first built in 1940, but the German Army's most widely-deployed wartime bike. Its sidecar drive had differential lock, two reverse and eight forward gears; its 26hp 750cc flat-twin engine gave the 420kg (926lb) three-wheeler, a 95km/h (59mph) top speed*
Below: *pricy but fast, the 1949 Vincent Series C Rapide's top speed was 177km/h (110mph) from its 998cc air-cooled four-valve pushrod 50-degree V-twin*

EVOLUTION AND HISTORY

One of the most successful postwar lightweights, which was to be produced in its thousands, was the BSA Bantam. Based on a DKW design and powered by a 123cc single-cylinder, two-stroke, three-speed engine, it featured petroil lubrication, fly-wheel magneto ignition, a solid rear subframe and undamped front telescopic forks, whereas the typical roadster of the period had no rear suspension, crude girder front forks, a bicycle-style single saddle and manual ignition.

During the 1950s, however, the British motorcycle industry grew complacent. It had gone from strength to strength with domestic sales reaching a peak of 330,000 in 1959, but by the early 1960s its failure to invest sufficiently in new engineering and design technology, coupled with its failure to recognise the need for change, to react to public demands, or to recognise competition, brought about its demise.

Below: *the last Douglas to be built was the beautiful 1957 Dragonfly model; after the war, the company had concentrated on what soon became its trademark 346cc ohv transverse mounted flat twin*

EVOLUTION AND HISTORY

Competition to the terribly dull British small-capacity bikes, which were mostly powered by Villiers two-stroke engines, had arrived by 1960 in the form of the 50cc NSU moped. It was followed by the onslaught of Italian Vespa and Lambretta scooters. Their step-through design was better suited to female riders, who could mount and dismount decorously even while clad in skirts and ordinary shoes. This section of the public had been totally ignored by the motorcycle manufacturers hitherto, yet for years would capture annual sales in excess of half a million. This was not all, for while the Italians became market leaders with their fashionable two-wheelers, there was the new challenge to be met of the four-wheel 850cc Mini car: thus within a short three-year period the combined effect upon the dominant British motorcycle industry was devastating.

In the USA, by now only Harley-Davidson remained. Indian had built its last big V-twin in 1953 and by the mid-1950s even Harley's sales had fallen below 10,000 units. By the 1960s Britain was faring little better. From 1954 the list of manufacturers that had ceased trading included OEC (1954); Wooler (1955); Douglas, Dunelt and Vincent (1956); Martin-Jap, New Hudson, Sunbeam and Tandon (1957); Norman (1961); Excelsior, Francis-Barnett and James (1964); P&M/Panther (1965), and Velocette (1968). AJS held on for a few precarious years although its range had been seriously curtailed since 1961; Matchless

Below: *Honda began production in 1947 with its A-Type auxiliary bicycle engine. The first bike to bear the Honda badge was the 98cc 1949 Dream D-Type*

EVOLUTION AND HISTORY

disappeared in 1969, and by 1971 these mystical names had been joined in the history books by still more famous names such as Ariel, BSA, and Royal Enfield.

The decline was felt not only in the UK and the USA, for across continental Europe and even in Japan consolidation saw the passing of many famous, long-established pioneering marques that included FN of Belgium (1957); Automoto of France (1962), and NSU of Germany (1965), which only a decade earlier had been producing nearly 25,000 bikes annually.

However, despite the universal despondency of the motorcycle world, a new revolution was in the making. Soichiro Honda had brought a batch of army-surplus two-strokes in 1946, for use in converting bicycles to mopeds. By 1949 Honda had developed his first motorcycle, and by 1951 he was selling 250 a week.

Part of Honda's success was that he did not rest on his laurels, as had the British. He developed a four-stroke as a stablemate for his two-stroke machine, went on to develop a step-through in 1952, and in the following year he completely re-tooled his factory. Despite facing bankruptcy, he vigorously continued to increase production of the 90cc four-stroke to 1,000 per month.

Honda visited the Isle of Man TT races in 1954 as a spectator, and returned in 1959 with his first race team. The following year at the TT, five of his six

Below: *Honda's 1969 four-cylinder Dream CB 750 Four established a benchmark of fine performance and sophistication at an affordable price*

Right: *the 740cc BSA Rocket was a three-cylinder ohv machine with a transverse-mounted engine that gave a top speed of 196km/h (122mph)*

decidedly uncomfortable and still basic 125cc machines finished the course. At the time his street machines were little different, except they they did come with what were for the time added extras such as wing-mirrors, flashing indicators, electric starters and toolkits; in Britain speedometers, brake lights and even pillion footrests were still optional extras. Thus it was not too long afterwards that Honda, along with the other Japanese manufacturers Suzuki and Yamaha, began to dominate the lightweight motorcycle market, as their competitors, particularly the British, were forced to close their doors.

It is easy with hindsight to criticise an expiring manufacturing industry, but the makers did not lose out to unfair competition as some claimed at the time; they disappeared like the dinosaurs because they did not develop, evolve, invest in or even understand the transport revolution and conditions that were taking shape under their noses, let alone on the broader horizon worldwide.

If mistakes had been made with the lightweights, then on the big bike front matters were worse, because manufacturers had been content to make slight modifications to existing designs. European offerings in the category were the results of overbored cylinder diameters to increase capacity, the addition of twin carburettors or modification of the camshaft profiles. The results were not basic street machines metamorphosed into sports models, but outdated designs that were inadequate to cope with the additional stresses and that delivered little, except discomfort and vibration.

Yet again it was Honda which revived a dispirited market, when in 1969 it launched the all-new CB750 with a four-cylinder ohc five-speed producing 67bhp. This Honda claimed to have put together from the drawing board to production in just six months, and was the harbinger of modern day motorcycling. Smooth, powerful and sophisticated, the CB750 (which was the first mass-produced four-cylinder bike) was undoubtedly in a different league to Britain's pushrod-engined Triumph T150 Trident, with its angular styling, kick start and drum brakes, or the BSA Rocket Three.

The CB750 heralded the start of motorcycling's modern age, and so the world in the 1970s belonged to the Japanese invaders, which included Kawasaki, Suzuki and Yamaha, in addition to Honda.

As the 1970s progressed, so did the supremacy and the products of the big four Japanese manufacturers, with a spate of unforgettably powerful machines such as the 900cc Kawasaki Z1, launched in 1973. It had a twin-cam engine that was capable of a top speed of 209km/h (130mph); by the end of the decade it had grown into the giant Z1300 six with echoes in the Suzuki GS1000, launched

EVOLUTION AND HISTORY

Below: the powerplant of the 1978 Suzuki GS1000 was an air-cooled eight-valve dohc transverse four which was based on that of Kawasaki, but the Suzuki outperformed the Z1 in almost every respect. It was capable of a top speed of 216km/h (135mph) from the 997cc unit, which produced 87bhp at 8,000rpm

EVOLUTION AND HISTORY

in 1978, and the Honda CBX1000, which was powered by a 1,047cc air-cooled 24-valve dohc transverse six. It was only then, in the 1970s, that as manufacturers finally learnt to apply the technology of the racetrack to the creation of the superfast road bikes, motorcycle design as well as the manufacturers' habits of thought began to be transformed.

Europe's response lay in the hands of the Italian manufacturers, and the distinctive V-twin engines of Ducati and Moto Guzzi, which in terms of handling still had the edge over the Japanese bikes. The Italians have continued to produce thrilling motorcycles such as the Ducati 750SS, a product of Italy's renowned design flair which became the ultimate escapist vehicle, but since the time of the launch of the CB750 the Japanese industry has been unquestionably the world's biggest, geared towards providing motorcycles for every market niche.

Below: *in the mid 1970s BMW launched its first-ever machine with a displacement greater than 750cc, the R90S, which was acknowledged as BMW's first superbike*

EVOLUTION AND HISTORY

Japanese dominance in the market place was prodigious; by the mid-1970s its production had reached 4.5 million units, compared to less than 800,000 in Italy and a meagre 40,000 in Great Britain. Japanese success continued throughout the industrialised West in the 1980s. Honda, Kawasaki, Suzuki and Yamaha were among the most heavily marketed and widely bought motorcycles, and they embodied the look and design of the era.

By the 1990s motorcycles were once again hot items. Designs like the Ducati M900, that in previous decades would never have been even mooted, were on the production line. This piece of pop culture, with high handlebars and an upright riding position, was not so much an Italian poser but more of a fashion statement from a house that also gave us the bike that Carl Fogarty rode to Superbike success, the highly desirable 916.

Above: *the Ducati M900 was like no other bike to have been produced, and it quickly became commonly known as Il Mostro (The Monster). The 904cc air/oilcooled sohc 90-degree Desmo V-twin unit has an output of 66.6hp at 7,000rpm and a top speed of 206km/h (128mph). So successful was the design that it spurred the design and production of other smaller versions; a 600 in 1994 with a 583cc unit, and a 750 in 1996 with a 748cc unit. There have also been a number of limited editions of the M900*

EVOLUTION AND HISTORY

So towards the end of the motorcycle's first century, there were encouraging signs of a revival from manufacturers outside Japan. In the UK, where 70,000 machines had still been manufactured yearly in the 1960s, there had been a dearth of bikes until the Triumph name was relaunched in 1992. In America, Harley had revived its fortunes on the back of a resurgence in nostalgia after it experienced severe financial problems in the 1980s, while in Germany BMW, which had proceeded from crisis to crisis in the postwar period, now emerged as the only significant survivor in the country that had given birth to the bike.

Below: *Triumph launched the Tiger 900 in 1993, as part of an exciting new range. The Tiger had a liquid-cooled, 3-cylinder 885cc 4-stroke dohc engine with 4 valves per cylinder, with a bore and stroke of 76 x 65mm (2.99 x 2.56in), and 3 x 36mm (1.42in) carburettors with a six-speed gearbox*

Right: *by the end of the century Harleys were fashionable again, even in the chic Paris locale of rue St-Honor*

EVOLUTION AND HISTORY

A CENTURY OF MOTORCYCLES

THE 1900s

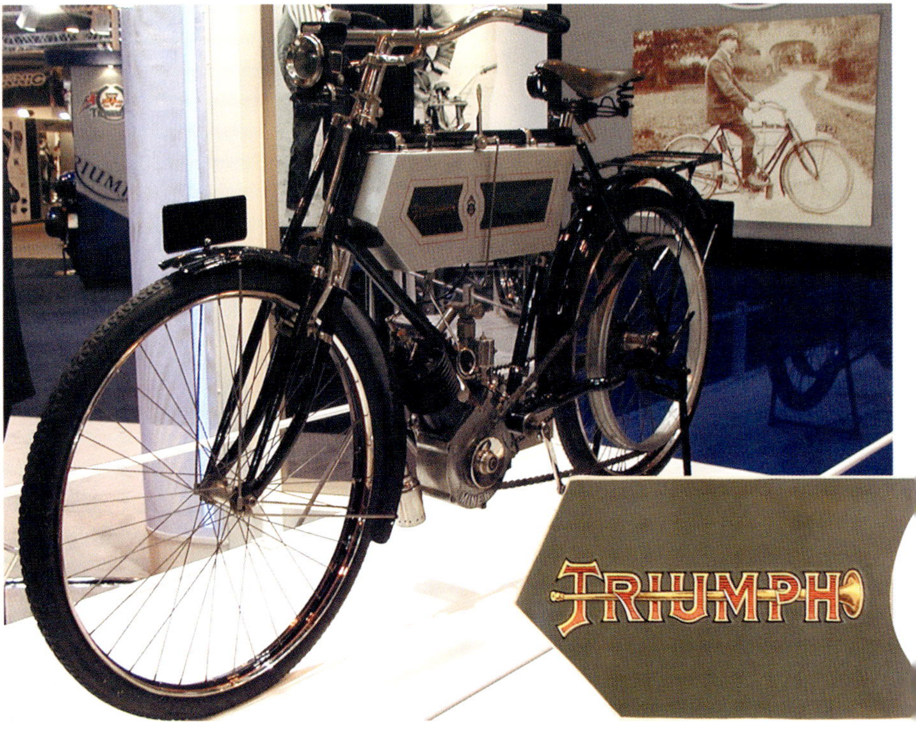

A CENTURY OF MOTORCYCLES

1901 *Facing page top left:* a Werner (France, 1897–1908) 1901 217cc
1902 *Facing page main picture centre, details top right and bottom right:* the first English-built Triumph in 1902 was powered by a 220cc Minerva engine
1903 *Above:* this 3hp 1903 Harley-Davidson (USA, 1903–) was the first motorcycle that the company sold
1904 *Above right:* Victoria (Germany, 1899–1966) originally fitted Zedel and Fafnir engines, then BMW units after the First World War. A 4.5hp 1904 machine with a Fafnir engine is illustrated
Centre right: Victoria's emblem
1905 *Below right:* one of the pioneer motorcycle producers Göricke (Germany) was established in 1903, and went on to built single and V-twin machines during the 1920s. One of its 1905 4.5hp V-twins is illustrated

A CENTURY OF MOTORCYCLES

1906 Above: by 1906 Triumph had its own 3hp engine, and the model illustrated also has rocking front forks
1907 Left: MCC (England, 1903–10) a short-lived company that started by fitting De Dion engines before producing its own using Minerva patents. Illustrated is one of the 1907 machines which has been beautifully restored
1908 Above right: a 493cc four-cylinder, shaft driven FN of 1908. FN was established in Belgium in 1901, a pioneer in the motorcycle field and for many years the leading make in Belgium. It was famous for using shaft drive between 1903 ands 1923. It ceased production in 1957
1909 Below right: Harley-Davidson introduced the V-twin in 1909, dropped it for the following year, and reintroduced it in the 7D in 1911

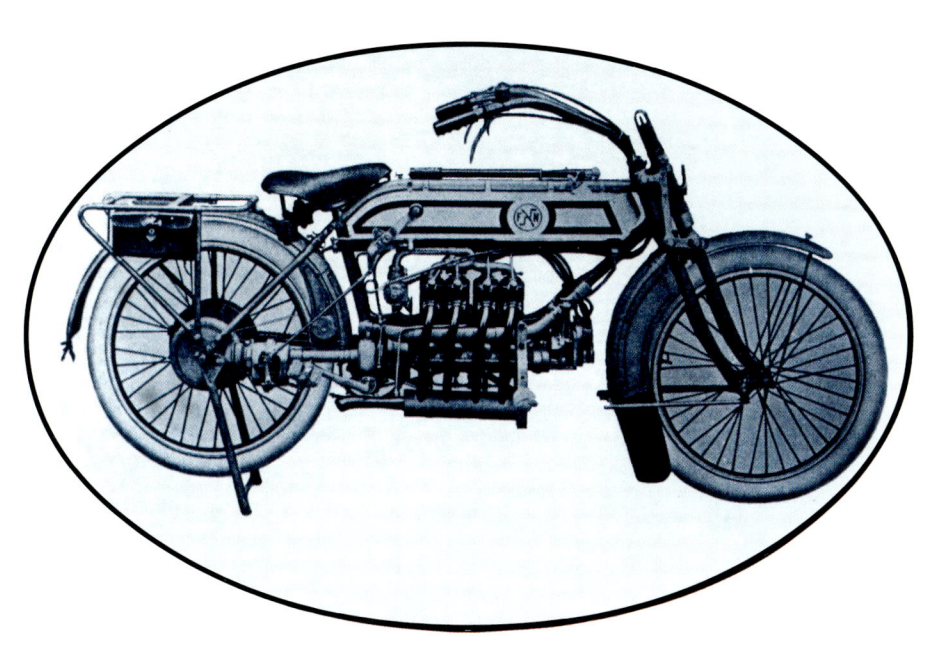

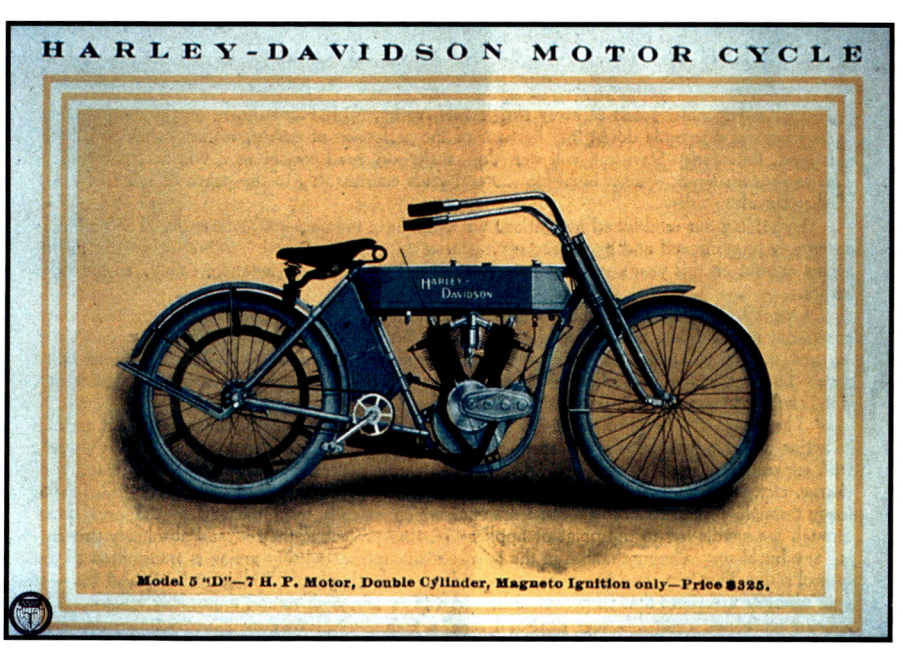

A CENTURY OF MOTORCYCLES

HARLEY-DAVIDSON MOTOR CYCLE

Model 5 "D"—7 H. P. Motor, Double Cylinder, Magneto Ignition only—Price $325.

A CENTURY OF MOTORCYCLES

THE 1910s

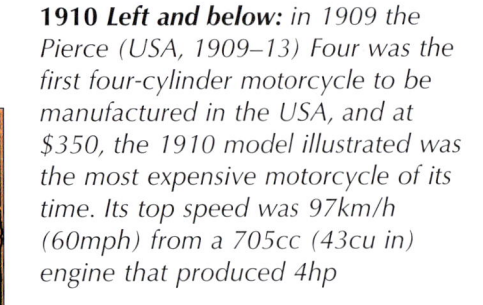

1910 Left and below: *in 1909 the Pierce (USA, 1909–13) Four was the first four-cylinder motorcycle to be manufactured in the USA, and at $350, the 1910 model illustrated was the most expensive motorcycle of its time. Its top speed was 97km/h (60mph) from a 705cc (43cu in) engine that produced 4hp*

36

A CENTURY OF MOTORCYCLES

1911 Bottom left: *FN (Belgium, 1901–57) had been the inspiration for the Pierce bike. The first FN machines were powered by 225cc and 286cc single-cylinder and 493cc and 748cc four-cylinder in-line engines. It was the first company to mass-produce a four-cylinder engine, and the example illustrated is from 1911, of a 493cc 8-valve four which had a top speed of only 64km/h (40mph)*

1912 Above: *the third of the four-cylinders to be illustrated in this section, and commonly regarded as the finest of them all, is the 1912 Henderson (USA, 1911–31). These motorcycles had air-cooled in-line unit-design engines with 1,068cc and 1,301cc*

1913 Right: *the 1913 Harley-Davidson catalogue cover*

37

A CENTURY OF MOTORCYCLES

1914 Left: *NSU (Germany, 1901–58) originally built machines powered by Swiss 1.5hp Zedel engines before building its own single-cylinder and V-twins. A 326cc model from 1914 is illustrated*

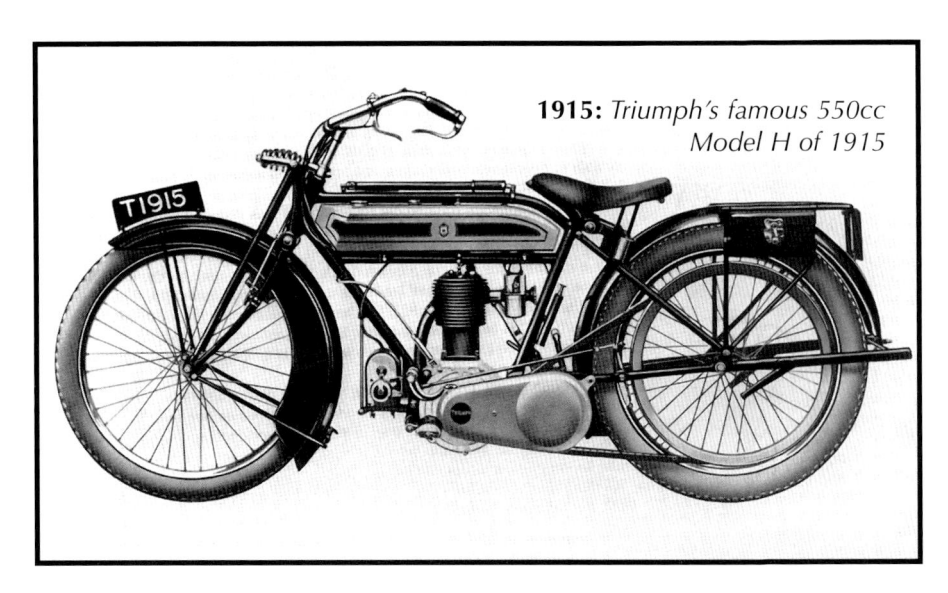

1915: *Triumph's famous 550cc Model H of 1915*

A CENTURY OF MOTORCYCLES

1916 Bottom left: Harley-Davidson's Service School was established in 1916 to train mechanics to service Army bikes

1917 Right: a 1,306cc machine from the short-lived Champion company (USA, 1911–18), from 1917

1918: a 998cc air-cooled 4-valve 42 degree V-twin was at the heart of this 1918 Indian Powerplus

1919: Harley's 35 Sport, introduced in 1919, used a flat twin

39

A CENTURY OF MOTORCYCLES

THE 1920s

1920: *after the First World War there were a lot of men unable to afford a car, in an era when it was also not the thing for a young lady to ride pillion. It was thus an ideal period for the sidecar, as promoted by the Triumph poster advertising the Gloria model,* **left**. *It was also in 1920 that William Walmsley built his first sidecar. The next year he moved to Blackpool where his neighborough was William Lyons. That same year they formed the Swallow Sidecar Company which became the Jaguar Car company* **1921:** *in April, Douglas Davidson became the first in England officially to exceed 100mph (160.9km/h), riding a Harley-Davidson.* **Right:** *Otto Walker on an eight-valve Harley, who averaged 168km/h (104.43 mph) in a 40.25km (25-mile) race at Beverly, California, in the same month*

1922 Below: *a non-production Opel (Germany, 1901–58) water-cooled track-racing machine with a 204cc ohv engine. The bike, ridden by Fritz von Opel and Philipp Karrer, also had a rearward-facing exhaust port and a big outside flywheel*

1923 Above: *Lorenz (Germany, 1921–25) retailed the Rapid, a 126cc two-stroke flat-twin engine which could be attached to a bicycle. The company also went into production to supply the complete machine*

A CENTURY OF MOTORCYCLES

1925 Below: another short-lived German company was Orionette (1921–25), which created a number of good two-stroke machines with mainly unit-design engines, including this 346cc bike which was not only its largest, but also its last

1924 Above: Sunbeam (England,1912–57) began by using JAP engines, but was building its own highly regarded singles by the mid-1920s, including this 492cc Longstroke sports version which had 77mm bore and 105mm stroke

A CENTURY OF MOTORCYCLES

42

A CENTURY OF MOTORCYCLES

1928: Indian became the largest bike manufacturer in the 1920s when it produced its highly successful Scout and Chief V-twins. The Big Chief, illustrated, had a 1200cc unit with a 42-degree cylinder angle

1926: well made and popular, the 498cc Hochland (Germany, 1926–27) flat-twin, **above left**, was unable to save the company from an early demise

1927: an original TT Norton, **below left**, beautifully maintained and still capable of turning in a highly creditable performance

1929: the Czechoslovakian company, Jawa, was formed in 1929, and its first machines were 497cc ohv shaft-driven bikes based on the German Wanderer design

43

A CENTURY OF MOTORCYCLES

THE 1930s

1930: Nestoria (Germany, 1926–27) took over the Astoria factory in 1925, after which it built 348cc and 498cc three-valve, single-cylinder ohc Küchen-engined machines before ending its production with the 496cc Sturmey-Archer engined bike, launched in 1930, **above**

1931: Indian built the W Henderson/ Arthur Lemon-designed 1265cc ACE machine from 1927, which eventually, after some design improvements, became the Indian-4, one of the most famous American motorcycles. **Below:** the 1931 model, with an air-cooled in-line four-cylinder 1200cc. It had side valves and 70mm bore and 83mm stroke

A CENTURY OF MOTORCYCLES

1932: *Austria's oldest motorcycle manufacturer, Püch, was established in 1903, when it manufactured motorcycles with its own small single-cylinder and V-twin engines. From 1923 it produced a series of double-piston two-strokes, including a 246cc model in 1932,* **right**

1933: *Motosacoche (MAG) (Switzerland, 1899–1957) began by developing a 215cc motorised bicycle at the beginning of the twentieth century. It had considerable success in the 1920s with 350cc and 500cc four-stroke singles, with its engines being at the heart of many successful race bikes. During the following decade sales dropped off and the company was forced to diversify. The last of its pre-war designs included the 496cc of 1933, illustrated* **above**

1934: *Imperia (Germany, 1924–35) was one of the many manufacturers to benefit from MAG engines, using 346cc, 496cc, 596cc, 746cc and 996cc power units. In the early 1930s Imperia relied upon four-valve ohv singles from both MAG and Bark, but when importation became difficult it decided to design its own air-cooled two-strokes, but money ran out before the engine was fully developed.* **Above** *is a 346cc model from 1934*

1935: *Garelli was founded in Italy in 1913, and become well known for its comprehensive range of mopeds and moto-cross machines. Its early history included double-piston two-stroke bikes wih 346cc engines which it developed until 1935. One of the last of these is illustrated* **left**

45

A CENTURY OF MOTORCYCLES

1936: Zündapp (Germany, 1917–85) was a major European producer, having manufactured 100,000 units by 1933 and 250,000 by 1942. It introduced a bike in 1933, illustrated **above**, with a pressed steel frame and a 798cc transverse-mounted flat four that produced 22bhp. It also produced a successful flat twin for the German troops in the Second World War, the KS750, but in peacetime concentrated on sporting bikes, which enabled the company to thrive during the 1960s and 1970s

1937: Ariel (England, 1902–70); originally the company was formed in Birmingham to build De Dion-engined three-wheelers; its well-known Square-Four was introduced in 1931. The factory also ceased production for a short period during the decade because of financial problems, but not before it had introduced the 248cc, 348cc and the powerful 498cc ohv Red Hunter range, illustrated **below left**

1938: Rudge-Whitworth (Rudge) (England, 1911–40) was an old-fashioned bicycle factory before going into motorbike manufacture. It first produced 499cc singles, but after the First World War produced a massive 749cc single with an 85mm bore and a 132mm stroke (3.35 x 5.20in), which it followed with an even bigger 998cc V-twin. Its first all-chain bike did not appear until the 1920s, when the singles still had belt drive to the rear wheel. In 1928 it won the Ulster Grand Prix, and named its sportiest model after that success; but official racing halted in the early 1930s, to be followed by the stoppage of racing machine production. By 1938 Rudge was in serious financial difficulties; its Coventry factory was sold, and the production of its most famous bike ended. **Top right:** one of its last bikes, a 499cc ohv four-valve Model Ulster from 1938, beautifully restored

1939: the year in which Triumph launched its Tiger 100, illustrated **bottom right**. This was a replacement for the sports single and was capable of reaching 160km/h (100mph); production was continued after the war

A CENTURY OF MOTORCYCLES

47

A CENTURY OF MOTORCYCLES

THE 1940s

1941–1946: *Zündapp ceased to supply civilian customers in 1940, but bikes such as the KS600, known as the Green Elephant, illustrated **below**, were reintroduced commercially in an improved form after the Second World War and remained in production until 1959*

1947: *Sunbeam, which had been absorbed into the BSA group in 1943, focussed on 487cc unit design engines after the war. Its S7 model, **right**, had shaft drive to the relatively small rear wheel and, along with the more sporty S8, was the last Sunbeam*

1948: *45cc Solex Vélosolex mopeds, **far right top**, remained a feature of postwar French streets for many years*

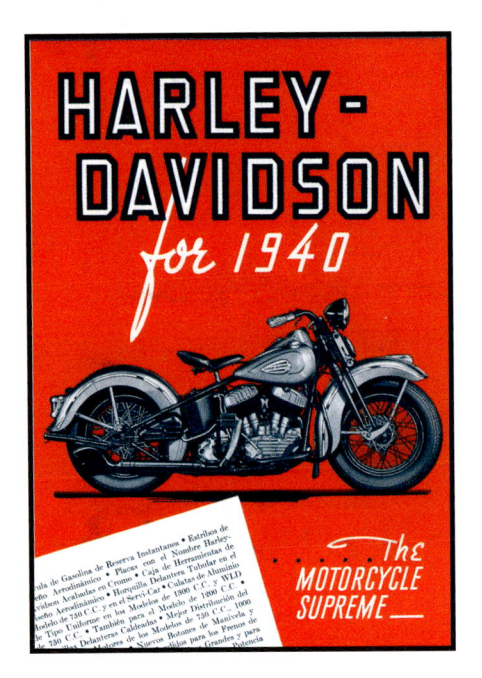

1940 Above: *the cover from the Harley-Davidson catalogue for 1940*

48

A CENTURY OF MOTORCYCLES

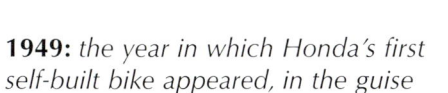

1949: *the year in which Honda's first self-built bike appeared, in the guise of the 98cc two-stroke model D, or Dream, illustrated **below***

49

A CENTURY OF MOTORCYCLES

THE 1950s

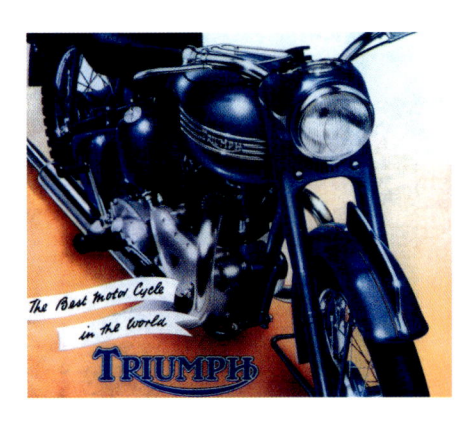

1950 Above: Triumph launched this 649cc Thunderbird model in 1950, the same year in which it introduced the four-bar tank logo
1951 Below: Moto Guzzi's Falcone Sport, with its horizontal single cylinder, was popular throughout the decade

1952: the first AJS appeared in 1909; in 1927 it introduced racing engines with chain-driven ohc and three-speed gearboxes, and built special engines for Brooklands races and a 996cc bike for an attempt on the world speed record. In 1931 the marque was sold to Matchless, and by the Second World War AJS was the fastest road racing machine being built. It became part of the BSA group in 1940, and of Associated Motor Cycles Ltd after the war. The AJS works racing team fared well postwar with 498cc twin-cylinder bikes, but in 1954 AJS withdrew from racing. The 1952 brochure, illustrated **above**, portrays its racing pedigree
1953: highly regarded as two-stroke specialists, DKW was founded in 1919, and by 1928 had become the world's largest motorcycle manufacturer. It merged with Audi, Horsch and Wanderer to form Auto Union AG in 1932, and enjoyed considerable racing success before the war. It was taken over by MZ postwar, before joining the Victoria and Express companies in 1957, in what became the Zweirad Union. This in turn was sold in 1966 to Fichtel & Sachs, which immediately dropped the name. The 1953 poster, illustrated **right**, promotes DKW's most famous machine, the RT 125, which had a 122cc two-stroke, three-speed engine

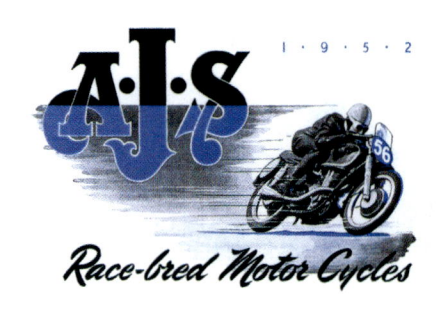

A CENTURY OF MOTORCYCLES

51

A CENTURY OF MOTORCYCLES

1954 Above: a 248cc Ilo-engined Hecker (Germany, 1921–56). Originally the company built its own 245cc two-strokes, but used Ilo and Sachs engines from 1945

1955: Vincent reintroduced 499cc singles in 1950, but it was its 998cc twins that won many races including the Clubman's TT, although works entries had ended in 1937; illustrated **below** is a Norvin Special

1956 Above: Norton introduced its parallel-twin 600cc engine, combined with the Featherbed frame to create the Dominator 99
1957 Above right: the MV Agusta Competizione was the Italian manufacturer's race version of its very popular 175CS, which was powered by a 174cc overhead-camshaft single-cylinder engine
1958 Below: Honda introduced a step-through type motorcycle, the Super Cub C 100, which provided easy and inexpensive transport
1959 Right: Triumph fitted twin carburettors to the T110 Tiger in 1959, to create the famous T120 Bonneville 650cc

A CENTURY OF MOTORCYCLES

A CENTURY OF MOTORCYCLES

THE 1960s

1960: *generally speaking, the decade was a good one for motorcycle sales but sadly it was also the last one for the British BSA (British Small Arms) marque. Established in 1906, it became England's leading motorcycle factory before its market was eroded by the Japanese invasion in the 1960s. Its reputation was made on the back of singles of simple and inexpensive design, built to provide everyday affordable transport. BSA was finally forced to close its doors in 1971. Its memorable post-war bikes include the Gold Star (497cc single-cylinder ohv model illustrated **below**), Golden Flash, Super Rocket, Clubman and Bantam models*

1961: *the decade was also the last for Matchless, which closed in 1969. The famous marque had been formed in the pioneering period in 1899, and had originally fitted De Dion engines to its models. In 1907 a JAP-engined Matchless won the very first TT race; it came second in 1908, first in 1909 and second again the following year. During the Second World War, the company produced large numbers of its 350cc single G3L model for the military. This became the G3LS in the 1950s, but the most famous Matchless was the G50 single-cylinder racer, which won many times throughout the 1960s. The G50, illustrated **above right**, was powered by an air-cooled two-valve SOHC single that produced 51bhp at 7,200rpm and was capable of a top speed of 217km/h (135mph)*

54

A CENTURY OF MOTORCYCLES

1962: Bianchi was yet another company, established in the nineteenth century, that failed to last through this decade. One of the foremost Italian pioneers, in the early days it produced motorised bicycles and cars, and by the 1930s Bianchi was most successful racing 350s. After the war its racing success continued with a variety of machines, from 123cc singles to 348cc twins; illustrated, **right**, is a 173cc ohc Sportster of 1962

1963: it all happened for Greeves in the 1960s. The company, formed in 1952, built mostly excellent off-road bikes that dominated moto-cross and scrambling events, winning the 250cc European Scrambling Championship in both 1960 and 1961. It ended the decade with a win in the Scottish Six Days Trial in 1969; illustrated **right** is a 1963 Villiers-engined 247cc model

A CENTURY OF MOTORCYCLES

1964 Above: *Triumph's Tiger 100; changing fashion had dictated the removal of the skirt over the rear wheel, a relic of 1957*

1965: *in addition to its single-cylinder Star models, BSA had introduced new 497cc and 646cc vertical ohv twins after the war. During the late 1960s it offered 441cc single-cylinder Victor and twin-cylinder Royal Star versions with 499cc engines as well as 654cc twins, which included the Thunderbolt, Lightning, Hornet and Spitfire models; a Lightning Clubman is illustrated* **above right**

56

A CENTURY OF MOTORCYCLES

1966: *this was the final year of the Triumph Twenty-One and Speed Twin models which included this smaller twin, illustrated* **below left**, *now also without its enclosing skirt, which had been introduced with the model in 1957*

1967: *Motorradwerke Zschopau (MZ) was established immediately after the Second World War in the DKW works in what was then East Germany. It grew to become one of the leading manufacturers in eastern Europe, enjoying considerable success in both trials and road races.*

Following German reunification MZ fell into financial trouble, but reappeared in 1994 as MuZ. Its best race results came in this decade; illustrated **above** *is the 248cc Model 250/1 G*

1968: *the first MV Agusta fours in production were sold from the late 1960s, and included the double overhead camshaft 600 model illustrated* **below**

57

A CENTURY OF MOTORCYCLES

1969: *BMW introduced a new range that included the R50/5, R60/5, and at the top of its range, the sporting 750cc R 75/5 machine, illustrated* ***below***. *The bikes featured new frames, improved telescopic forks and ohv engines of 498, 598 and 746cc and were released as a challenge to the rejuvenated bikes being prepared by the Japanese manufacturers*

A CENTURY OF MOTORCYCLES

A CENTURY OF MOTORCYCLES

THE 1970s

1970 Right: the catalogue cover for the Norton Commando, a 745cc twin that had been launched in the previous year, and which for a time was able to hold off the Japanese invaders by virtue of its superior handling. Production of the Commando ended in 1977

1971 Below: an advertisement that heralds the introduction of the Harley-Davidson Super Glide; an exciting combination of parts from the Electra Glide and Sportster ranges, it had a 1,200cc engine and was capable of 188km/h (117mph). Little wonder then, that it sold nearly 5,000 units in its first year

1972 Above right: the Triumph Trident was given new forks and hubs in 1971, the following year went over to a five-speed gearbox, and in the year after that received disc front brakes. This was the period in which the British motorcycle industry also underwent a period of severe change and concentration, which ended with virtually all mass production in one group. This group, comprising BSA, Norton Villiers and Triumph, produced two famous surviving marques: Norton, produced at Wolverhampton, and Triumph, produced at the Meriden factory. This left the Small Heath, Birmingham, factory to produce Triumph Trident engines. The

A CENTURY OF MOTORCYCLES

rationalisation programme decided upon in September 1973 included the closure of the Meriden factory, and the end of production for the new Bonneville. After eighteen months of negotiations and a government grant and loans, production of the Bonneville was continued under a workers' co-operative. A further government loan in May 1977 enabled the co-operative to buy the rights for the Triumph Trident

1973: the first big motorcycle factory in Spain was that of Montesa, which was established in Barcelona immediately after the Second World War. Initially it concentrated on 124cc two-stroke machines with which it achieved many successes in races during the 1950s, and went on to win the world trials championship in 1980. Since the 1980s it has used Honda engines; illustrated, **above right**, is a 247cc King Scorpion

1974: two new Laverda 744cc ohc twins appeared in 1974; illustrated **below** is the 750 SFC

A CENTURY OF MOTORCYCLES

1975: *the BMW R 90 S first appeared in 1973, and was the first BMW machine displacing more than 750cc. The 1975 version, with its characteristic cockpit fairing and 67bhp sports engine, is illustrated* **above**

1976: *in the mid-decade Ducati was producing its Desmo roadsters, the fastest and the best singles. They were complemented by Ducati's first V-twin, the 750GT that appeared in 1971; a 842cc V-twin (the 1976 version is illustrated* **centre right***), and in 1976 by a potent 900 Super Sport. Arguably the greatest Italian sportster of the period, this was capable of 230km/h (144mph) from its four-valve sohc 90-degree V-twin*

1977: *Kawasaki had launched its Z1 in 1973; this four-cylinder superbike ioriginally had a 903cc transverse engine. It was renamed the Z900 in 1976, and a year later the engine was enlarged to 1,015cc to produce the Z1000, illustrated* **below**

A CENTURY OF MOTORCYCLES

1978 Right: BMW's smallest production Boxer to date, the R 45, came with an engine displacement of 473cc. This machine was introduced mainly for the 27bhp insurance category in Germany, the unrestrained engine developing 35bhp

1979 Below: the Triumph Bonneville Special appeared in 1979, with cast-alloy wheels and an all-black finish with gold lining, but it did nothing to halt the decline of a factory that was slowly running out of both money and time

THE 1980s

1980 *Below:* this was the year that Triumph introduced its Executive model), in the search for a new customer base. It came with fairing, panniers and a top box as standard. Another new model, the Royal, was introduced in the following year to celebrate the wedding of Prince Charles and Princess Diana

1982: the first American Dirt Track Championship took place in 1954, with races taking place on ovals or TT-style courses which featured both jumps and bends. The Harley rider Scott Parker is illustrated **below**, in 1982. Parker retired in 1999 after recording 93 career wins, including nine National Championships

1981: also saw the introduction by Triumph of the Trial model, but none of its efforts could halt the slow decline of Triumph. Illustrated **above right** is the 744cc Tiger Trial, which was first shown at the Paris show as a 1981 model; later, a 649cc version was built. Meriden production ceased in 1983, and inevitably the company went into receivership and was sold off. The factory that had produced so many memorable bikes was sadly demolished

A CENTURY OF MOTORCYCLES

1984: *the Frenchman Hubert Auriol won the gruelling Paris-Dakar Rally for a second time, in 1983. Auriol had first won the event in 1981 when riding a modified BMW R 80 G/S bike. His feat was equalled by his colleague and co-BMW works rider, the Belgian Gaston Rahier in 1984 and 1985. Both riders are shown,* **below left**, *celebrating after the 1983 Rally win; Hubert Auriol is the rider on the left*

1983: *the sixtieth anniversary of BMW motorcycles was celebrated when the company launched a new concept on the world market. This was an all-new K-series with a water-cooled straight-four power unit fitted in a flat longitudinal arrangement. Illustrated* **above** *are the K 100, K 100 RS and the K 100 RT*

1985: *the year in which BMW set up a new production record also saw the range of its K Series enlarged with the addition of the 750cc three-cylinder K 75 C model, illustrated* **above**. *The Series had been introduced in October 1983 in the form of the unfaired K 100, the half-faired K 100 RS sports, and the fully-faired K 100 RT touring models, all of which were powered by a DOHC 987cc water-cooled, fuel-injected four-cylinder engine*

A CENTURY OF MOTORCYCLES

8,000rpm and delivers a top speed of nearly 241km/h (150mph)

1989: the former road-racer Erik Buell left Harley-Davidson, where he was employed as an engineer, in 1983 and founded the Buell Motor Company. His first bike was the RR1000, which had some success in twin-cylinder races in mid-decade, but in 1989 he launched the RS1200, illustrated **below right**, which was powered by the Harley Sportster V-twin mounted in Buell's tubular steel ladder Uniplaner frame. Harley-Davidson purchased 49 per cent of the company in 1993, and it was renamed Buell Motorcycle Company in the following year

1986: when Triumph went into liquidation, the name was bought by John Bloor. He licensed Racing Spares, which was already producing Triumph spares, to build the Bonneville as produced in its final form only, for a period of five years. Illustrated **above** is one of its bikes made in 1986, for the US market

1987: a new era dawned for Benelli in 1971 when it was taken over by the late Alejandro De Tomaso, and its new flagship bike appeared in 1974. Unfortunately the six-cylinder 750cc Benelli Sei caused more people to gasp at its price than its styling. It was followed by a slightly more powerful 900, illustrated **right**, but this went out of production in 1987
1988 Above right: the 1988 brochure for the Yamaha V-Max, which had been first introduced in 1985. The big four had caused a sensation, but not for its looks; it is completely dominated by its engine, a water-cooled DOCH 16-valve 1,198cc V-four that produces 145bhp at

A CENTURY OF MOTORCYCLES

A CENTURY OF MOTORCYCLES

THE 1990s

1990: *during the 1990s Moto Guzzi continued to produce an impressive range of powerful bikes that included the Daytona 1000 (1992), 1100 Sport (1994), its top-selling California (1994), and at the very beginning of the decade, illustrated* **above,** *the stylish Nevada 750 (1990)*

1991: *a radical sportster, the Bimota Testi 1D, illustrated* **below**, *was available in 1991, with a distinctive hub-centre front suspension arrangement. Sadly, Bimota went into liquidation and its assets were sold off at the end of 2001*

1992: *Wayne Gardener, illustrated* **right**, *astride a Rothmans-Honda NSR500 V-four during the 1992 500cc World Championship*

1993: *following the success of its rearranged 900SS in 1991, Ducati put that 904cc sohc 90-degree Desmo V-twin engine into a brutally-styled, unfaired bike, the M900 Monster, illustrated* **below right**

1994: *Kawasaki's superbike of the era was the ZZ-R1100, illustrated* **overleaf**. *Its awesome 145bhp water-cooled 16-valve, dohc, 1,052cc transverse four was capable of a top speed of 280km/h (175mph)*

68

A CENTURY OF MOTORCYCLES

A CENTURY OF MOTORCYCLES

A CENTURY OF MOTORCYCLES

A CENTURY OF MOTORCYCLES

A CENTURY OF MOTORCYCLES

A CENTURY OF MOTORCYCLES

A CENTURY OF MOTORCYCLES

1995: *Aprilia's RS250, illustrated on the **previous pages**, was built as a replica of its 1994 250cc World Championship bike, ridden by Max Biaggi. Also launched in this year was its radically-styled Moto' 6.5, illustrated **above left**, a truly striking and innovative machine designed by Philippe Starck*

1996: *BMW had introduced the R 1100 RS in 1993 to celebrate the 70th anniversary of the Boxer, and followed it with its largest and most powerful machine to date, the K 1200 RS sports tourer, illustrated **below left**. It was in the same year, 1996, that BMW decided to halt the production of its long-established K 75 model*

1997: *the quintessential Harley-Davidson is the Ultra Classic Electra Glide, illustrated **above right**. Launched in 1965, at a time when Harley's share of the US market had dropped to a mere six per cent, it has grown to be the epitome of the American motorcycle. The new model, which followed almost immediately the company went public, was in effect the Duo Glide with an electric start. The Electra Glide, through upgrading and modification, has remained the most dreamed about, and sought-after, fully-accessorised touring model*

1998 Right: *behind the quad exhausts of the MV Agusta F4 lies a liquid-cooled dohc 750cc engine with a Weber-Marelli electronic fuel and injection system*

75

A CENTURY OF MOTORCYCLES

A CENTURY OF MOTORCYCLES

1999: *the end of the century, but it ended on a high note for Triumph. In 1991 when the reborn Triumph factory emerged on the world stage, it established its credentials with the Trident and Trophy models. The Daytona 1200, its response to the Japanese superbikes, followed. At its heart is a water-cooled dohc 16-valve in-line 1,180cc four, which was geared to a top speed of only 257km/h (160mph), but this was still Britain's fastest-ever production motorcycle and certainly established the street cred of the reborn marque*

MOTORCYCLE ANATOMY

Brakes: a lever near the hand grip controls the front wheel, which today is usually of the hydraulic disc type, apart from on the very small bikes which use drum brakes. The rear brake may be disc or drum, and is engaged by a foot pedal. Several manufacturers have now developed successful, although expensive, anti-lock or ABS systems

In the drum brake method, a pair of semi-circular shoes is forced open against the inside of the drum when the brake is applied.

The disc brake system comprises a single steel disc, which is gripped by the twin pads of a hydraulically-operated calliper.

Clutch and throttle: these control the engine speed, and are operated by twist-type controls on the hand-grips.

Engines: generally produced with either two-stroke or four-stroke cycles, with up to four cylinders. Most are air-cooled, though a few are water-cooled. Single-cylinder motorcycles usually have four-stroke petrol engines, with the smaller machines, below 250cc, utilising two-stroke engines which are mechanically simpler, cheaper to produce and more economical to run, although they need more frequent decarbonization. They are also normally limited to 1,200cc (73 cubic in) displacements, with the highest performance levels in racing attained by the superbikes with up to 160 horsepower produced for vehicles weighing approximately 227kg (500lbs).

The two-stroke's workings are more complex than those of the four-stroke engine, because instead of having mechanical valves a two-stroke uses the underneath of the piston to force the incoming mixture of fuel and air into the combustion chamber via the crankcase and connecting transfer ports. The engine is thus able to fire with every rotation of the crankcase; the drawback to this is that the lubricating oil cannot sit in the crankcase, and must be carried in the fuel/air mixture and burnt.

Parallel twins have been the favoured layout of many manufacturers and are used by Yamaha in its RD350LC; whereas Kawasaki has recently favoured tandem twins with one cylinder behind the other, Aprilia, together with many of the 250cc Grand Prix bikes, uses in-line V-twins.

Two-stroke triples have been used by Kawasaki in its H1 and H2 bikes, along with the Suzuki GT750, and a V-triple appeared in the Honda NS500 and NS400.

Four-cylinder two-strokes have been used by Honda, Suzuki and Yamaha, especially for recent 500cc

MOTORCYCLE ANATOMY

Grand Prix bikes; the Honda NSR500 has just a single crankshaft.

The four-stroke engine, named after its four basic operations of induction, compression, combustion and exhaust, was invented by Dr Nikolaus Otto (1832–91), and its principle has been motorcycling's mainstay throughout its history.

The earliest and simplest four-stroke layout, the single, reaches its practical limitation at about 650cc, but it dominated during the middle of the century until the 1960s, when it was superceded by parallel twins. These have the design flexibility of being able to be used either in 180-degree or in 360-degree layout, where both pistons rise together. Twins can be flat like the BMW Boxer, V like Harley-Davidson's 45-degree layout or Ducati's 90-degree version, or transverse as for Moto Guzzi. The background illustration on these pages is of the 2002 Buell Firebolt XB9R, which has at its heart a Harley-Davidson 984cc four-stroke 45-degree V-twin.

Three-cylinder engines can be arranged either across the frame like Triumphs, or along the line like the BMW K75, though many manufacturers now use the Japanese-favoured transverse format as for the Honda CB750.

Five-cylinder bikes have been unfashionable for many years, but the Honda GL1,500 Gold Wing has a water-cooled SOHC horizontally-opposed flat-six, while the same manufacturer uses a straight-six to power its CBX1000.

Rotary engines are the smoothest-running, however, but are high on fuel consumption. Invented by Felix Wankel (1902–88) in 1956, this engine is based on a three-sided rotor contained within a figure-of-eight chamber, the rotor turning in such a way that its corners always remain in contact with the sides.

The European method of rating an engine is by the volumetric displacement of the pistons in cubic centimetres. The horsepower method of rating is used in the United States. A rough equivalent is 8 to 10 horsepower per 100 cubic cm.

Frame: these are most often of steel, and usually a combination of sheets and tubes are used; however graphite and magnesium parts are becoming more common because of their high strength-to-weight characteristics. Until the middle of the century the majority of bikes had thin steel frames, with damperless or simple friction springer front forks. There was also a considerable lack of rear suspension, the rider's comfort being provided by a sprung saddle. Hydraulically damped rear shock absorbers (where oil is forced through holes of various sizes) were introduced in the 1960s, when the engine was also sometimes used as an integral stressed member, as with the Honda four-cylinder racers.

The rear shock absorbers work in much the same way as the front

79

MOTORCYCLE ANATOMY

forks, absorbing the shocks with a coil spring and using a haudraulic damper to control the rate of the compression.

The chassis differs according to the type of bike; for instance, a modern race bike is designed with a short wheelbase, steep front forks, and the weight loaded over the front wheel to provide light steering for a quicker response. A tourer, however, is designed with a long wheelbase to increase stability, has raked forks and a lot of tail, giving more weight over the rear wheel.

In between the racer and the tourer is the roadster, with its adjustable fork rakes and various methods to fine-tune both the front and rear suspension.

Starter: the kick start has been mostly replaced by an electric push-button starter; for the larger machines a coil-ignition electrical system is used, and on the smaller, lightweight two-strokes a magneto ignition is common

Suspension: provided by coil springs on a telescopic fork at the front, and springs, often mounted on shock absorbers similar to those used on an automobile, at the rear.

Transmissions: typically four to six speeds, although some of the smaller bikes have as few as two. Power is normally transmitted to the rear wheel sprockets via a chain or gearing between engine and gearbox and then by primary chain. In some of the more advanced machines the final drive is via a shaft and bevel-gear system.

Tyres: smaller than those used for most automobiles, and also rounder to permit leaning, which on modern bikes can be in excess of 45 degrees, to lower the centre of gravity in a turn without the loss of traction.

Tyres of large cross-section, containing air at relatively low pressure and known as balloon tyres, were common during the 1920s. Before the Second World War, beaded-edge tyres became popular; this pneumatic tyre had an outer covering with a hard edge or beading to fit into a channel at each side of the wheel rim.

Most bikes had tubed front and rear tyres of similar size and of crossply construction, until the 1960s. Today's superbikes need soft-compound, low profile, tubeless radial tyres, and wear a much wider rear tyre to cope with the extreme power demands.

Wheels: generally comprise aluminium or steel rims with spokes, although some cast wheels, which began to be favoured in the 1970s, are used. These are normally made of aluminium, but stronger, lighter materials such as magnesium are also available.

Today's superbikes have been standardised with a 43.18cm (17-inch) diameter wheel front and rear, although at different times a 40.64cm (16 inch) front has been fashionable.

John Boyd Dunlop (1840–1921)

Born in Strathclyde, Dunlop was a flourishing veterinary surgeon with a practice near Belfast, when he invented the pneumatic tyre, first used for bicycles, in about 1887. His company, formed in 1889, became known as the Dunlop Rubber Company in 1900.

Above: Suzuki's new DL1000 V-Strom is the manufacturer's all-new concept of a versatile, multi-purpose adventure sportsbike, and was introduced for 2002

MODERN MOTORCYCLES

MODERN MOTORCYCLES

This chapter is designed to feature as many of the current models as practicable, together with their main technical specifications

Above: *Aprilia's 2002 six-speed RSV Mille R model*

APRILIA

The company, which was formed in Italy in 1968, began by producing 123cc Sachs and Hiro-engined two-strokes for trials and moto-cross, together with a range of 49cc machines. Such was its develoment that in recent years it has grown to become one of the world's most dynamic manufacturers, winning both the 250cc and the 125cc world titles in 1994. Today's range includes a replica model of the 1994 RS racebike, together with the RSV, Falco, Caponord, Futura, Pegaso and RX models, plus a big range of scooters.

MILLE R

Engine type: liquid-cooled, four-stroke, twin-cylinder with 4 valves per cylinder
Bore x stroke: 97 x 67.5mm (3.82 x 2.66in)
Displacement: 997.62cc
Brakes: front, 320mm (12.6in) diameter disc; rear, 220mm (8.66in) disc
Tyres: front, 120/65 ZR 431.8mm (17in) or 120/70 ZR 431.8mm (17in); rear, 180/55 ZR 431.8mm (17in) or 190/50 ZR 431.8mm (17in)
Dry weight: 185kg (407.93lb)

FALCO R

Engine type: liquid-cooled, four-stroke, 60° longitudinal V-twin
Bore x stroke: 97 x 67.5mm (3.82 x 2.66in)
Displacement: 997.62cc
Compression ratio: 10.4 :1
Transmission: six-speed
Maximum power output: 72kw (98hp) at 8,250rpm
Ignition: digital electronic with two spark plugs per cylinder (TSI Twin Spark Ignition), integrated with injection. Electronically-controlled Dynamic Ignition Advance Control (DIAC)
Starter system: electric
Lubrication: dry crankcase with separate oil reservoir; double trochoidal pump with oil cooling radiator
Primary drive: straight tooth gear, transmission ratio: 60/31 (1.935)
Frame type: double sloping curved beam frame (Double Wave Twin Beam) in box-type aluminium-magnesium alloy, removable steel saddle mount
Wheels: Tubeless Spokes Rim (patented); front, 63.5 x 482.6mm (2.50 x 19in); rear, 101.6 x 431.8mm (4.00 X 17in)
Clutch: multiple disc in oil bath with servo-assisted hydraulic control (PPC patent); Freudenberg clutch tubing
Brakes: front, stainless steel 300mm (11.81in) diameter Brembo double floating disc. Twin pot floating callipers, differentiated diameter (32 and 30mm / 1.26 and 1.18in) and pads of semi-metallic material. Freudenberg brake tubing; rear, stainless steel 270mm (10.63in) diameter disc. Twin pot calliper, 34mm (1.34in) diameter Freudenberg brake tubing
Tyres: tubeless radial; front, 110 / 80 VR 482.6mm (19in); rear, 150 / 70 VR 431.8mm (17in)
Suspension: front, hydraulic Marzocchi fork, 50mm sleeves, wheel travel 175mm (6.89in); rear, swing arm in aluminium alloy, progressive linkage with Aprilia Progressive System (APS). Sachs hydraulic shock absorber, adjustable in brake in rebound and preload. Wheel travel, 185mm (7.28in)
Fuel tank: 25 litres (5.5Imp gal / 6.6US gal), including 5 litre (1.1Imp gal / 1.32US gal) reserve
Measurements: overall length 2,310mm (90.94in); width (at handlebars) 830mm (32.67in); height (at fairing) 1,440mm (56.69in); wheelbase 1,560mm (61.42in); seat height 820mm (32.28in)
Dry weight: 215kg (474lb)

Left: the Falco R SL 1000, illustrated in Aprilia's Plumb Grey

CAPONORD

Engine type: liquid-cooled, four-stroke 60° longitudinal V-twin
Bore x stroke: 97 x 67.5mm (3.82 x 2.66in)
Displacement: 997.62cc
Compression ratio: 10.4 :1
Starter: electric
Brakes: front, stainless steel 300mm (11.81in) diameter Brembo double floating disc; rear, stainless steel 270mm (10.63in) diameter disc
Tyres: tubeless radial; front, 110 / 80 VR 482.6mm (19in); rear, 150 / 70 VR 431.8mm (17in)
Fuel tank: 25 litres (5.5Imp gal / 6.6US gal), including 5 litre (1.1Imp gal / 1.32US gal) reserve
Dry weight: 215kg (474lb)

Below: Aprilia's new CapoNord ETV 1000

FUTURA

Engine type: liquid-cooled, four-stroke, longitudinal 60° V twin
Bore x stroke: 97 x 67.5mm (3.82 x 2.66in)
Displacement: 997.62cc
Compression ratio: 11.4:1
Starter: electric
Transmission: six-speed
Frame type: sloping double parallel lateral beam frame in box-type aluminium-magnesium alloy
Suspension: front, Showa upside-down fork, 43mm (1.69in) diameter sleeves, adjustable in brake, rebound and preload, 120mm (4.72in) wheel travel; rear, swing arm in aluminium alloy, progressive linkage with Aprilia Progressive System (APS). Sachs hydraulic shock absorber, adjustable in brake, rebound and preload. Wheel travel, 120mm (4.72in)
Fuel tank: 21 litres (4.62Imp gal / 5.54US gal)
Seat height: 820mm (32.28in)
Dry weight: 215kg (474lb)

Above: the Futura RST 1000, a true sport-touring bike specifically designed for fast, high-performance touring

APRILIA

PEGASO

Engine type: four-stroke, single-cylinder
Bore x stroke: 100 x 83mm (3.94 x 3.27in)
Displacement: 651.8cc
Compression ratio: 9.1 : 1
Output: 36kW (49hp) at 6250rpm
Transmission: five-speed
Frame type: sloping aluminium double beam
Fuel tank: 21 litres (4.62Imp gal / 5.54US gal)
Measurements: overall length 2180mm (85.83in); width (at half-handlebars) 920mm (36.22in); height (at front fairing) 1260mm (49.61in); wheelbase 1475mm (58.07in); seat height 810mm (31.89in)
Dry weight: 175kg (385.88lb)

Above right: the restyled single-cylinder Pegaso I E 650 enduro, which has been oriented more towards touring, and now features a lower saddle height

RX 50

The Aprilia RX 50, illustrated *below left*, represents the perfect compromise between technology and excitement. It is the ideal first motorbike for those wanting to combine a desire for freedom with practical everyday use, designed with free time in mind, but to the highest possible technical standards. It features a two-stroke, liquid-cooled engine and six-ratio gearbox to ensure above-average performance, the fruit of Aprilia's long racing traditions. It also has excellent handling in all situations and riding conditions. The attractive frame is made from high-tensile tubular steel with closed-cradle split at the level of the exhaust. Both front and rear discs combine to ensure complete safety.

87

BMW

BMW entered the new millenium on a high by delivering nearly 75,000 units in the year 2000, its eighth successive record production year. In the past twelve months it has capitalized further on its success with the introduction of more new models than ever before. It added the R 1150 R, the R 1150 RT and the K 1200 RS in March 2001, and at the end of the year introduced the truly outstanding F 650 CS single-cylinder and the R 1150 RS Sports Tourer. BMW's range is now the youngest that it has ever been, as the R 1200 C which was introduced in the autumn of 1997 currently the oldest model in the range.

The all-new funduro F 650 GS, launched in the spring of 2000, was the first successor model in the F Series range, and the first single-cylinder in the world to be equipped with Digital Motor Electronics and a fully-controlled catalytic converter. It is also now available with ABS as an option. The F 650 CS model that followed introduced a world-first achievement in motorcycle construction with the combination of a single swinging arm and a toothed drive belt.

Below: *from 2002 the F 650 GS Dakar was also available with ABS anti-lock brakes, which can be deactivated by the rider if required, but the model is only available in the desert blue/aura white colour combination*

K 1200 RS

Engine type: water-cooled, four-cylinder, four-stroke in line with four valves per cylinder
Bore x stroke: 70.5 x 75mm (2.78 x 2.95in)
Displacement: 1171cc
Output: 96kW (130hp) at 8750rpm
Transmission: six-speed
Tyres: front, 120 / 70 ZR 431.8mm (17in) tubeless; rear, 170 / 60 ZR 431.8mm (17in) tubeless
Wheels: light alloy
Frame type: cast aluminium, vibration decoupled engine
Suspension: BMW Telelever with longitudinal strut located centrally in the frame
Fuel tank: 21 litres (4.62Imp gal / 5.54US gal)
Measurements: seat height 770mm (30.3in), 800mm (31.5in)
Dry weight: 285kg (628lb)
Maximum speed: 200km/h (124mph)

Below: originally introduced in 1997, the K 1200 RS Sports Tourer has been updated to improve touring comfort with the inclusion of BMW's new EVO brake on the front wheel

R 1150 GS

Engine type: water / oil-cooled, two-cylinder, flat twin with four valves per cylinder
Bore x stroke: 101 x 70.5mm (3.98 x 2.78in)
Displacement: 1130cc
Output: 62.5kW (84.5hp) at 6750rpm
Transmission: six-speed, including overdrive-type sixth gear which is now featured as standard
Tyres: front, 110 / 80 R 431.8mm 482.6mm (19in) 59H tubeless; rear, 150 / 70 R 431.8mm (17in) 69H tubeless
Wheels: cross spoke
Frame type: three-piece front; rear frame with monocoque engine / gearbox unit
Suspension: BMW Telelever with control spring strut, spring pre-tension with four fold adjustment and tilt decoupling
Fuel tank: 21.1 litres (4.64Imp gal / 5.57US gal)
Dry weight: 228kg (503lb)
Maximum speed: 193km/h (120mph)

R 1150 RS

Engine type: water / oil-cooled, two-cylinder, four-stroke flat twin with four valves per cylinder
Bore x stroke: 101 x 101mm (3.98 x 3.98in)
Displacement: 1130cc
Output: 70kW (95hp) at 7250rpm
Transmission: five-speed
Tyres: front, 120 / 70 ZR 431.8mm (17in) tubeless; rear, 170 / 60 ZR 431.8mm (17in) tubeless
Wheels: light alloy
Frame type: three piece front, rear frame with monocoque engine / gearbox unit
Suspension: BMW Telelever with central swing strut with infinitely variable tension adjustment
Fuel tank: 23.1 litres (5.08Imp gal / 6.09US gal)
Measurements: seat height 790mm (31.1in), 810mm (31.9in), 830mm (32.7in)
Dry weight: 246kg (542lb)
Maximum speed: 200km/h (124mph)

BUELL

Buell has become Harley-Davidson's sports bike arm, and in 2001 launched the ultra-radical XB9R Firebolt, its first Sport Fighter bike. Its aggressive looks and sports dynamics completed the marque's 2002 three-model range.

LIGHTNING X1 / WHITE LIGHTNING X1W

Engine type: air-cooled, ohv 45° four-stroke V-twin with two valves per cylinder
Bore x stroke: 88.8 x 96.8mm (3.5 x 3.8in)
Displacement: 1,203cc
Compression ratio: 10.0 :1
Output: 71kW (95hp) at 6200rpm
Transmission: five-speed
Brakes: front, 340mm (13.39in) diameter floating disc; rear, 230mm (9.06in)
Measurements: overall length 2070mm (81.5in); width 760mm (29.9in); height 1170mm (46in); wheelbase 1410mm (55.5in); seat height 749mm (29.5in); ground clearance 125mm (4.9in)
Dry weight: 200kg (440lb)

CYCLONE M2

Engine type: air-cooled, ohv 45° four-stroke V-twin with two valves per cylinder
Bore x stroke: 88.8 x 96.8mm (3.5 x 3.8in)
Displacement: 1,203cc
Compression ratio: 10.0 :1
Output: 70kW (93.5hp) at 6100rpm
Transmission: five-speed
Brakes: front, 340mm (13.39in) diameter floating disc; rear, 230mm (9.06in)
Tyres: front, Dunlop D 250 F Sportmax Tour 120 / 70 ZR 431.8mm (17in); rear, Dunlop D 250 Sportmax Tour 170 / 60 ZR 431.8mm (17in)
Measurements: overall length 2050mm (80.7in); width 800mm (31.5in); height 1140mm (44.9in); wheelbase 1410mm (55.5in); seat height 749mm (29.5in); ground clearance 132mm (5.2in)
Dry weight: 197.3kg (435lb)

Below left: the Lightning X1, which is capable of 217km/h (135mph)
Below right: Buell's M2, unlike the X1, does not have fuel injection

MODERN MOTORCYCLES

FIREBOLT XB9R

Engine type: air-cooled, ohv 45° four-stroke V-twin with two valves per cylinder
Bore x stroke: 88.8 x 79.8mm (3.5 x 3.125in)
Displacement: 984cc
Compression ratio: 10.0 :1
Output: 69kW (92hp) at 7200rpm
Transmission: five-speed
Brakes: front, 375mm (14.76in) diameter floating disc; rear, 230mm (9.06in)
Tyres: front, Dunlop D 270 FY Sportmax 120 / 70 ZR 431.8mm (17in); rear, Dunlop D 270 Y Sportmax 180 / 55 ZR 431.8mm (17in)
Measurements: overall length 1924mm (75.75in);
width 768mm (30.25in); height 1092mm (43in);
wheelbase 1320mm (52in);
seat height 775mm (30.5in);
ground clearance 127mm (5in)
Dry weight: 175kg (385lb)

Below: the Firebolt contains many unusal design features; the frame holds fuel, the light alloy swing-arm holds oil, and the front brake, which is on the rim perimeter, attaches to the wheel rim

MODERN MOTORCYCLES

CAGIVA

Now united with the equally famous motorcycle marques of MV Agusta and Husqvarna, the group represents a formidable force in the industry and it is to be hoped that it enjoys the success that its technical brilliance deserves.

The Cagiva range for model year 2002 comprised the Navigator, **above left**; the Planet, **far left**; the Mito, **left**; and the Raptor, which along with the V Raptor is available with either 650cc or 1000cc engines. **Right:** the 1000cc V Raptor

DUCATI

The year 2001 was Ducati's seventy-fifth anniversary year, and to celebrate the occasion Troy Bayliss, on a factory Ducati Infostrada, won the World Superbike Championship. This was the manufacturer's ninth riders' title in fourteen years, and it also took the manufacturers' title.

In September of 2001, Ducati announced the introduction of the Multistrada 1000, a new-generation sport bike intended to deliver a combination of sportbike performance, design, and all-road abilities. The current Ducati range also includes the 998, the bullish Monster, the Supersport, and the Sporttouring.

998R

Engine type: liquid-cooled, twin-cylinder Desmodromic, four valves per cylinder
Bore x stroke: 104 x 58.8mm (4.09 x 2.31in)
Displacement: 999cc
Compression ratio: 12.3 :1
Output: 102kW (139hp) at 10,000rpm
Transmission: six-speed

DUCATI

MULTISTRADA 1000

Engine type: air-cooled, twin-cylinder Desmodromic, two valves per cylinder
Bore x stroke: 94 x 71.5mm (3.7 x 2.81in)
Displacement: 992cc
Transmission: six-speed
Frame type: tubular steel trellis
Suspension: front, upside-down fork; rear, progressive linkage
Brakes: front, pair of 320mm (12.6in) diameter semi-floating discs; rear, 245mm (9.65in) diameter single disc
Tyres: front, 120 / 70 ZR 431.8mm (17in); rear, 190 / 50 ZR 431.8mm (17in)
Dry weight: 212kg (467lb)

Left: the 998 with its Testastretta engine replaced Ducati's 996 as its flagship superbike
Above: the Multistrada has been designed to excel in all road riding conditions; it is a quality sport bike which has the flexibility of a big enduro for the real enthusiast

900 SPORT

Engine type: air-cooled, twin-cylinder, with two valves per cylinder
Bore x stroke: 92 x 68mm (3.62 x 2.68in)
Displacement: 904cc
Compression ratio: 9.2:1
Output: 59kW (80hp) at 7500rpm
Transmission: six-speed
Brakes: front, 320mm (12.6in) diameter double disc; rear, 245mm (9.65in) diameter single disc
Measurements: overall length 2030mm (79.9in); height 1100mm (43.3in); wheelbase 1395mm (54.9in); seat height 815mm (32.1in)
Dry weight: 188kg (414lb)

Below: the 900 and 750 Supersport models have five-spoke wheels, whereas the Sport models, including the 900 Sport illustrated, have three-spoke wheels. The range is available with either full or half fairing
Right: the Sporttouring range was launched in 1997; an ST4 is illustrated

SPORTTOURING ST4

Engine type: liquid-cooled, twin-cylinder, with four valves per cylinder
Bore x stroke: 98 x 66mm (3.86 x 2.6in)
Displacement: 996cc
Compression ratio: 11.5:1
Output: 86kW (117hp) at 8750rpm
Transmission: six-speed
Brakes: front, pair of 320mm (12.6in) diameter semi-floating discs; rear, 245mm (9.65in) diameter single disc
Tyres: front, 120 / 70 ZR 431.8mm (17in); rear, 180 / 55 ZR 431.8mm (17in)
Frame type: tubular steel trellis
Suspension: front, Showa upside-down fork, 43mm (1.69in) diameter; rear, progressive linkage with Öhlins fully-adjustable monoshock
Fuel tank: 21 litres (4.62Imp gal / 5.54US gal)
Measurements: overall length 2070mm (81.5in); height 1180mm (46.5in); wheelbase 1430mm (56.3in); seat height 820mm (32.3in)
Dry weight: 212kg (467lb)

GILERA

When Piaggio announced the closure of the Gilera Arcore factory in 1993, it was thought that henceforth the famous racing name would only be found adorning scooters, but in 2001 the famous marque was back in the international motorcycle arena with the launch of the Gilera Supersport 600. The engine is from Suzuki's GSX-R600, but the rest is pure Italian. The Gilera range is completed by the innovative DNA motorcycle-style scooter and the new ICE 50cc street scooter.

DNA

Engine type: liquid-cooled, four-stroke, four valve
Displacement: 125cc
Output: 11kW (15hp) at 9700rpm
Tyres: front, 120 / 70 355.6mm (14in); rear, 140 / 70 355.6mm (14in)
Fuel tank: 9 litres (1.98Imp gal / 2.37US gal)
Measurements: overall length 1870mm (73.6in); width 520mm (20.5in); wheelbase 1330mm (52.4in); seat height 770mm (30.3in)

SUPERSPORT 600

Engine type: liquid-cooled, four-stroke, four-cylinder, dohc
Bore x stroke: 67 x 42.5mm (2.64 x 1.67in)
Displacement: 599cc
Starter: electric
Transmission: six-speed
Brakes: front, 320mm (12.6in) diameter dual Brembo discs; rear, 220mm (8.66in) diameter single disc
Tyres: front, 120 / 70 ZR 431.8mm (17in); rear, 180 / 55 ZR 431.8mm (17in)
Frame type: twin beam combining light alloy and titanium elements
Suspension: front, fully adjustable, upside-down, 43mm (1.69in) diameter shafts; rear, swing arm, progressive linkage, single shock absorber, fully adjustable
Fuel tank: 18 litres (3.96Imp gal / 4.75US gal)
Measurements: overall length 2000mm (78.7in); width 715mm (28.1in); height 1135mm (44.7in); wheelbase 1392mm (54.8in); seat height 830mm (32.7in)
Dry weight: 162kg (357lb)

Below left: *the DNA 125, which is also available in a 180cc, 20hp version and as a 50cc GP Experience model*
Below: *Gilera's comeback bike, the superlight, superfast Supersport 600*

HARLEY-DAVIDSON

From a small wooden shed, via near-bankruptcy, the American motorcycle icon is one hundred years old in 2003. By then Harley, the world's biggest manufacturer of heavyweight (over 650cc) motorcycles, will be selling in excess of 250,000 motorcycles per year in Europe and will finally have outsold Honda in its own domestic market for the first time for a third of a century.

The Harley-Davidson stable now cosists of 23 bikes across five styles ranging from the Sportster, introduced in 1957, to the V-Rod, launched in July 2001.

XL53C CUSTOM 53 (SPORTSTER)

Engine type: air-cooled, ohv, 45-degree V-twin
Bore x stroke: 76.2 x 96.8mm (3.0 x 3.81in)
Displacement: 883cc
Compression ratio: 9.0:1
Measurements: overall length 2245mm (88.4in); wheelbase 1510mm (59.4in); seat height 700mm (27.6in); ground clearance 159mm (6.3in)
Dry weight: 245kg (540lb)

HARLEY-DAVIDSON

FXDL LOW RIDER (DYNA GLIDE)

Engine type: air-cooled, Twin Cam 88, V-twin
Bore x stroke: 95.3 x 101.6mm (3.75 x 4.0in)
Displacement: 1449cc
Compression ratio: 8.8:1
Transmission: five-speed
Brakes: front, 292mm (11.5in) diameter discs; rear, 292mm (11.5in) diameter discs
Tyres: front, 100 / 90 482,6mm (19in) 57H; rear, 150 / 80B 406.4mm (16in) 71H
Fuel tank: 18.5 litres (4.07Imp gal / 4.88US gal)
Measurements: overall length 2330mm (91.7in); wheelbase 1620mm (63.8in); seat height 640mm (25.2in); ground clearance 117mm (4.6in)
Dry weight: 300kg (662lb)

Below left: the latest Sportster Custom features tall forks, a sleek twin seat, chromed bullet headlight and indicators, combined with forward foot controls and a laced front wheel. However, as for many Harleys, it is the Evolution V-twin that really impresses
Below: a long, low, raked Harley in the form of the 2002 model Dyna Low Rider

FLSTF/I FAT BOY (SOFTAIL)

Engine type: air-cooled, Twin Cam 88B, V-twin
Bore x stroke: 95.3 x 101.6mm (3.75 x 4.0in)
Displacement: 1449cc
Compression ratio: 8.8:1
Transmission: five-speed
Brakes: front, 292mm (11.5in) diameter discs; rear, 292mm (11.5in) diameter discs
Tyres: front, MT90B 406.4mm (16in) 72H; rear, MT90B 406.4mm (16in) 74H
Fuel tank: 18.9 litres (4.12Imp gal / 4.95US gal)
Measurements: overall length 2396mm (94.3in); wheelbase 1630mm (64.2in); seat height 647mm (25.5in); ground clearance 123mm (4.8in)
Dry weight: 320kg (706lb)

Below: this is Harley-Davidson's heavyset, big-boned Fat Boy, complete with giant headlight and solid disc wheels encased in fat rubber tyres. At the centre of this machine is the big Twin Cam 88B, launched in 1998 and now counterbalanced and available in carb or sophisticated electronic fuel injection (EFI). Harley's seven-strong Softail range, all of which have similar engines to that above, comprises the Standard, Night Train, Fat Boy (illustrated), Springer, Deuce, Heritage Classic and Heritage Springer

HARLEY-DAVIDSON

FLHTC ELECTRA GLIDE CLASSIC (TOURING)

Engine type: air-cooled, Twin Cam 88, V-twin
Bore x stroke: 95.3 x 101.6mm (3.75 x 4.0in)
Displacement: 1449cc
Compression ratio: 8.8:1
Transmission: five-speed
Brakes: front, dual 292mm (11.5in) diameter discs; rear, 292mm (11.5in) diameter discs
Tyres: front, MT90B 406.4mm (16in) 72H; rear, MT90B 406.4mm (16in) 74H
Fuel tank: 18.9 litres (4.12Imp gal / 4.95US gal)
Measurements: overall length 2500mm (98.4in); wheelbase 1592mm (62.7in); seat height 693mm (27.3in); ground clearance 130mm (5.1in)
Dry weight: 345kg (761lb)

Below: the Electra Glide was introduced in 1965, and has retained its traditional looks into the new millenium

HONDA

Acclaimed by many as the finest motorcycle ever made, Honda's VFR800Fi was completely overhauled for 2002 (*illustrated right*), to include fuel injection V-TEC valve engineering. This improves engine performance by utilising a unique two-stage valve control system, effectively combining the benefits of both two-valve (at lower speeds) and four-valve (at higher speeds) systems.

The renowned Japanese racing pedigree includes over 500 GP wins, eleven 500cc World Championships and 13 Constructors, plus 113 Isle of Man TT wins. For 2002 Honda produced a number of race-ready 600cc Supersport machines based on the CBR600F Sport model, in a package that included spare wheels, a limited spares kit, data sheets, set-up information, and an initial test day with advice from Honda's world championship team to assist with base settings.

Honda's comprehensive current range also includes the Fireblade, launched in 1992; the now more powerful Pan European; the naked Hornet CB900F with its mono-backbone steel frame, and the new four-stroke CRF450R motocross/supercross bike (*illustrated below*). In addition, there is the VTR1000SP-2, the successor to the bike on which, in its debut year, Colin Edwards won the world's 2000 Superbike Championship (he was to finish second in the following year).

VFR800FI

Engine type: liquid-cooled, four-stroke, 16-valve, dohc 90 degree V-4
Bore x stroke: 72 x 48mm (2.83 x 1.89in)
Displacement: 781.7cc
Compression ratio: 11.6:1
Output: 80kW (108bhp) at 10,500rpm
Starter: electric
Transmission: six-speed
Brakes: front, 296mm (11.65in) diameter dual floating hydraulic disc; rear, 256mm (10.08in) diameter single hydraulic disc
Tyres: front, 120 / 70 ZR 431.8mm (17in)M/C (58W); rear, 180 / 55 ZR 431.8mm (17in) M/C (73W)
Suspension: front, 43mm (1.69in) diameter HMAS cartridge-type telescopic fork with stepless preload adjustment; rear, Pro-Link with gas-charged HMAS damper, seven-step preload and stepless rebound damping adjustment
Fuel tank: 22 litres (4.84Imp gal / 5.81US gal)
Measurements: overall length 2120mm (83.5in); width 735mm (28.9in); height 1195mm (47.0in); wheelbase 1460mm (57.5in); seat height 805mm (31.7in); ground clearance 130mm (5.1in)
Dry weight: 213kg (470lb)

MODERN MOTORCYCLES

FIREBLADE

Engine type: liquid-cooled, four-stroke, 16-valve, dohc inline-4
Bore x stroke: 75 x 54mm (2.95 x 2.13in)
Displacement: 954cc
Compression ratio: 11.5:1
Output: 111kW (150bhp) at 11,250rpm
Starter: electric
Transmission: six-speed
Brakes: front, 330mm (13.00in) diameter dual disc; rear, 220mm (8.66in) diameter single-piston calliper disc
Tyres: front, 120 / 70 ZR 431.8mm (17in); rear, 190 / 50 ZR 431.8mm (17in)
Suspension: front, 43mm (1.69in) diameter inverted HMAS cartridge-type telescopic fork with stepless preload, compression and rebound adjustment; rear, Pro-Link with gas-charged HMAS damper, 13-step preload and stepless compression and rebound damping adjustment
Fuel tank: 18 litres (3.96Imp gal / 4.76US gal)
Measurements: overall length 2065mm (81.3in); width 680mm (26.8in); height 1125mm (44.3in); wheelbase 1400mm (55.1in); seat height 815mm (32.1in)
Dry weight: 168kg (370lb)

HONDA

HORNET CB900F

Engine type: liquid-cooled, four-stroke, 16-valve, dohc inline-4
Bore x stroke: 71 x 58mm (2.80 x 2.28in)
Displacement: 919cc
Compression ratio: 10.8:1
Output: 81kW (109bhp) at 9,000rpm
Starter: electric
Transmission: six-speed
Brakes: front, 296mm (11.65in) diameter dual hydraulic disc; rear, 240mm (9.45in) diameter single hydraulic disc
Tyres: front, 120 / 70 ZR 431.8mm (17in) M/C (58W); rear, 180 / 55 ZR 431.8mm (17in) M/C (73W)
Suspension: front, 43mm (1.69in) diameter cartridge-type telescopic fork; rear, monoshock damper with seven-step adjustable preload
Fuel tank: 19 litres (4.18Imp gal / 5.02US gal)
Measurements: overall length 2125mm (83.7in); width 750mm (29.5in); height 1085mm (42.7in); wheelbase 1460mm (57.5in); seat height 795mm (31.3in); ground clearance 145mm (5.7in)
Dry weight: 195kg (430lb)

PAN EUROPEAN

Engine type: liquid-cooled, four-stroke, 16-valve, dohc 90 degree V-4
Bore x stroke: 78 x 66mm (3.07 x 2.60in)
Displacement: 1,261cc
Compression ratio: 10.8:1
Output: 87kW (118bhp) at 8,000rpm
Starter: electric
Transmission: five-speed
Brakes: front, 310mm (12.20in) diameter dual hydraulic disc; rear, 316mm (12.44in) diameter single hydraulic disc
Tyres: front, 120 / 70 ZR 457.2mm (18in); rear, 170 / 60 ZR 431.8mm (17in)
Suspension: front, 45mm (1.77in) diameter air-assist telescopic fork; rear, single-side conventional damper with adjustable preload
Fuel tank: 29 litres (6.38Imp gal / 7.66US gal)
Measurements: overall length 2282mm (89.8in); width 935mm (36.8in); height 1332mm (52.4in); wheelbase 1500mm (59.1in); seat height 790mm (31.1in); ground clearance 145mm (5.7in)
Dry weight: 276kg (609lb)

VTR1000 SP-2

Engine type: liquid-cooled, four-stroke, 8-valve, dohc 90 degree V-twin
Bore x stroke: 100 x 63.6mm (3.94 x 2.50in)
Displacement: 999cc
Compression ratio: 10.8:1
Output: 99kW (134bhp) at 10,000rpm
Starter: electric
Transmission: six-speed
Brakes: front, 350mm (13.78in) diameter dual hydraulic disc; rear, 220mm (8.66in) diameter hydraulic disc
Tyres: front, 120 / 70 ZR 431.8mm (17in) (58W); rear, 190 / 50 ZR 431.8mm (17in) (73W)
Suspension: front, 43mm (1.69in) diameter inverted cartridge-type fork; rear, Pro-Link with gas-charged integrated remote reservoir damper offering adjustable preload, compression and rebound damping
Fuel tank: 18 litres (3.96Imp gal / 4.76US gal), including 2.5 litre (0.55Imp gal / 0.66US gal) warning light reserve
Measurements: overall length 2025mm (79.7in); width 725mm (28.5in); height 1120mm (44.1in); wheelbase 1420mm (55.9in); seat height 820mm (32.3in); ground clearance 140mm (5.5in)
Dry weight: 194kg (428lb)

KAWASAKI

Kawasaki's current line-up comprises over twenty models. They range from the new 64cc KX65 (*illustrated right*) youth motocross bike to the aggressively-styled, low-riding 1,470cc-powered VN1500 Mean Streak performance cruiser, and from the basic Eliminator to the awesome new Ninja ZX-12R supersports machine.

Andrew Pitt, *below*, took the 2001 FIM World Supersport Championship 600 on a factory Ninja ZX-6R. The Ninja range, which represents an extremely cohesive rider/machine relationship, is improved upon as the new Nine, which has over 130 modifications, including a completely redesigned frame and engine mounting method. The Kawasaki flagship, the phenomenal XZ-12R, has had its awesome power harnessed with the benefit of Ram Air technology.

When the ZZ-R1100 sports tourer was introduced in 1990, it was named Machine of the Year by NMC. Its direct decendant, the ZZ-R1200, was announced in 2001 with an 1164cc engine that has a lightweight all-aluminium cylinder block and a bank of CVKD40 Keihin carburettors, and it has that look about it which suggests that it will become as legendary as its ancestor.

Also new for 2002 was the Retro W650; modified as a café racer, this is a bike with bite and attitude. It has a big aluminium fuel tank, low seat, high footpegs, low-slung handlebars and swept-back exhaust pipes.

KX65

Engine type: liquid-cooled, two-stroke, 4-valve, single
Bore x stroke: 44.5 x 41.6mm (1.75 x 1.64in)
Displacement: 64cc
Compression ratio: 8.4:1
Output: 12.3kW (16.7bhp) at 12,500rpm
Transmission: six-speed
Brakes: front, 180mm (7.09in) single disc; rear, 180mm (7.09in) single disc
Tyres: front, 60 / 100 355.6mm (14in) diameter (30M); rear, 80 / 100 304.8mm (12in) diameter (41M)
Suspension: front, 33mm (1.30in) telescopic fork; rear, bottom-link Uni-Trak
Measurements: overall length 1590mm (62.6in); width 760mm (29.9in); height 995mm (39.2in); wheelbase 1120mm (44.1in); seat height 760mm (29.9in); ground clearance 305mm (12in)
Dry weight: 57kg (126lb)

VN1500 MEAN STREAK

Engine type: liquid-cooled, four-stroke, 8-valve, sohc V-twin
Bore x stroke: 102 x 90mm (4.02 x 3.54in)
Displacement: 1,470cc
Compression ratio: 9.0:1
Output: 53 kW (72bhp) at 5,500rpm
Starter: electric
Transmission: five-speed
Brakes: front, 320mm (12.60in) diameter semi-floating dual discs; rear, 300mm (11.81in) diameter single disc
Tyres: front, 130 / 70 R 431.8mm (17in) M/C (62H); rear, 170 / 60 R 431.8mm (17in) M/C (72H)
Suspension: front, 43mm (1.69in) diameter inverted telescopic fork; rear, swing arm with twin shocks
Fuel tank: 17 litres (3.74Imp gal / 4.49US gal)

Measurements: overall length 2,410mm (94.9in); width 850mm (33.5in); height 1,100mm (43.3in); wheelbase 1,705mm (67.1in); seat height 700mm (27.6in); ground clearance 125mm (4.9in)
Dry weight: 289kg (637lb)

KAWASAKI

MODERN MOTORCYCLES

W650

Engine type: air-cooled, 8-valve, parallel twin-cylinder
Displacement: 676cc
Transmission: five-speed
Brakes: front, single disc; rear, drum
Frame type: double cradle
Fuel tank: 15 litres (3.30Imp gal / 3.96US gal)
Measurements: wheelbase 1455mm (57.28in); seat height 800mm (31.45in)
Dry weight: 195kg (430lb)

Above and below: the W650, which is also now available in Retro version

ELIMINATOR 125

Engine type: air-cooled, 2-valve single-cylinder
Displacement: 124cc
Transmission: five-speed
Brakes: front, single disc; rear, drum
Tyres: front, 90 / 90 431.8mm (17in) diameter; rear, 130 / 90 381mm (15in) diameter M/C
Suspension: telescopic forks and twin shock absorbers with adjustable preload

Frame type: double cradle
Fuel tank: 13 litres (2.86Imp gal / 3.44US gal)
Measurements: wheelbase 1470mm (57.87in); seat height 680mm (26.77in)
Dry weight: 135kg (297lb)

Above: Kawasaki's entry motorcycle is the Eliminator, a perfectly balanced and affordable everyday machine that is practical, economical and comes with a proven pedigree from a manufacturer that has been in business now for over fifty years

KAWASAKI

ZXR400

Engine type: liquid-cooled, 16-valve in-line four-cylinder
Displacement: 398cc
Transmission: six-speed
Tyres: front, 120 / 60 R 431.8mm (17in) diameter; rear, 160 /60 R 431.8mm (17in) diameter
Suspension: 41mm (1.61in) upside-down telescopic forks and Uni-Trak both with rebound damping plus adjustable preload

ZZ-R1200

Engine type: liquid-cooled, 16-valve, four-cylinder
Displacement: 1,164cc
Transmission: six-speed
Brakes: front, semi-floating twin discs; rear, single disc
Frame type: aluminium perimeter style
Fuel tank: 23 litres (5.06Imp gal / 6.08US gal)
Measurements: wheelbase 1505mm (59.25in); seat height 800mm (31.50in)
Dry weight: 236kg (520.38lb)

Above and below: Kawasaki's superbike

Brakes: front, semi-floating twin discs; rear, single disc
Frame type: aluminium, perimeter style
Fuel tank: 16 litres (3.52Imp gal / 4.23US gal)
Measurements: wheelbase 1385mm (54.53in); seat height 790mm (31.10in)
Dry weight: 162kg (357lb)

Above: the smaller-engined version of the well-mannered machine that has won just about everything

KTM

KTM bikes took first, second, third, fourth and fifth places in the 2001 Dakar Rally, to add to its World Enduro Championship and World Motorcross Championship titles, representing a very impressive list of achievements for the Austrian company that was founded in 1953.

The company grew quickly in its early years, winning its first event in 1954, to become one of Europe's leading factories, based on the production of 98cc Rotax-engined two-strokes. It also produced 49cc mopeds and scooters. Attention was later switched to concentrate almost exclusively on trials and moto-cross machines using Puch and Sachs engines, before entering into production of its own 173cc, 246cc, 346cc and 355cc two-stroke engines. These were to power its machines to many victories in both trials and moto-cross, and later also enduro events.

In 1991 KTM went into liquidation, but re-emerged soon afterwards under new management, since when it has gone from strenght to strength.

Its current sports motorcycles range from 50–950cc and encompass Roadsters in addition to the wide selection of moto-cross, enduro and sports mini-cycles.

KTM

380 SX

Engine type: liquid-cooled, single-cylinder, two-stroke
Bore x stroke: 78 x 77mm (3.07 x 3.03in)
Displacement: 368cc
Starter: kickstart
Transmission: five-speed
Brakes: front, 260mm (10.24in) diameter disc; rear, 220mm (8.66in) diameter disc
Tyres: front, 80 / 100 46.4mm (21in); rear, 110 / 90 44.4mm (19in)
Frame: chromium-molybdenum, powder coated
Fuel tank: 7.5 litres (1.65Imp gal / 1.98US gal)
Measurements: wheelbase 1481mm (58.31in); seat height 925mm (36.42in); ground clearance 385mm (15.16in)
Dry weight: 101kg (223lb)

Below left: KTM's desert racing version of the 950 Rally, which is powered by its new dohc 942cc V-twin

Below right: the 380 SX is just one of KTM's five-model SX motorcross range

MOTO GUZZI

In the 1980s Moto Guzzi produced a range of V-Twins that lagged behind the Japanese bikes in terms both of performance and price, but by the early 1990s the Guzzies were back and there was a renaissance of the Italian motorcycle. Its first new high performer was the Daytona 1000, powered by an air-cooled sohc 8-valve fuel-injected 992cc V-twin that made the bike capable of a genuine 233km/h (145mph). Moto Guzzi followed the Daytona with the bigger 1100 Sport, with its pushrod-operated transverse V-twin engine.

In parallel to the high performance motorcycles of the 1990s, the company evolved touring bikes such as the California series. Now, owned by Aprilia since 2000 and with a new production line, the range encompasses both of these spirits of sport and touring, in the legendary California series, the traditional Nevada, and the aggressive 1100 V in Sport Naked and Le Mans versions.

Below: *the evergreen Nevada 750 has been on the market for over a decade*

MOTO GUZZI

CALIFORNIA STONE

Engine type: air-cooled, four-stroke, dohv 90 degree V-twin
Bore x stroke: 92 x 80mm (3.62 x 3.15in)
Displacement: 1,046cc
Compression ratio: 9.5:1
Output: 54kW (73bhp) at 6,400rpm
Starter: electric
Transmission: five-speed
Brakes: front, 320mm (12.60in) diameter Brembo floating disc; rear, 282mm (11.10in) diameter fixed disc
Tyres: front, 110 / 90 VB 457.2mm (18in); rear, 140 / 80 VB 431.8mm (17in)
Frame: detachable tubular duplex cradle in special high-strength steel
Suspension: front, 45mm (1.77in) diameter telescopic fork; rear, swing arm with two hydraulic shock absorbers
Fuel tank: 19 litres (4.18Imp gal / 5.02US gal)
Measurements: overall length 2355mm (92.72in); width 850mm (33.46in); height 1150mm (45.28in); wheelbase 1560mm (61.42in); seat height 760mm (29.92in)
Dry weight: 246kg (542lb)

LE MANS

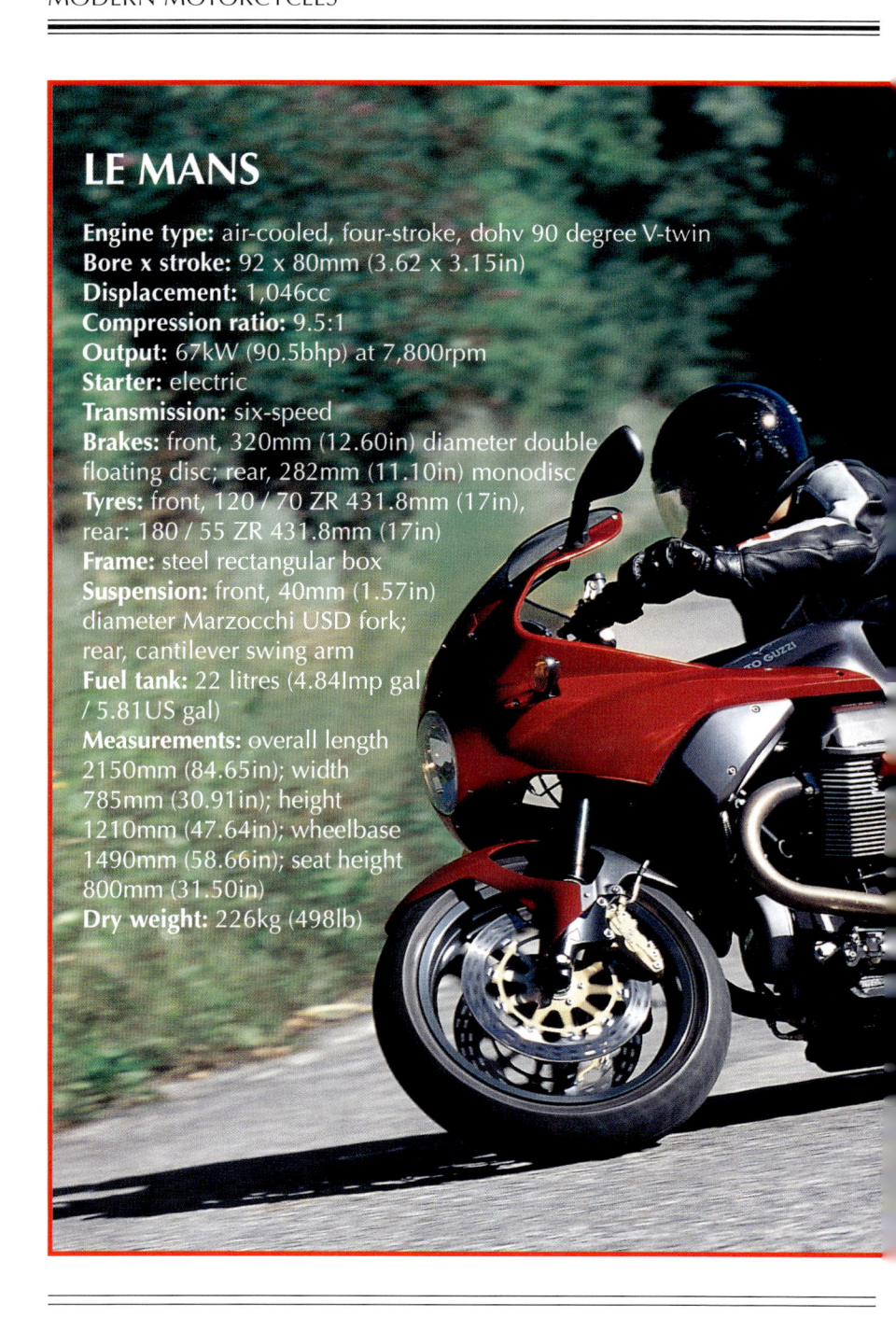

Engine type: air-cooled, four-stroke, dohv 90 degree V-twin
Bore x stroke: 92 x 80mm (3.62 x 3.15in)
Displacement: 1,046cc
Compression ratio: 9.5:1
Output: 67kW (90.5bhp) at 7,800rpm
Starter: electric
Transmission: six-speed
Brakes: front, 320mm (12.60in) diameter double floating disc; rear, 282mm (11.10in) monodisc
Tyres: front, 120 / 70 ZR 431.8mm (17in), rear: 180 / 55 ZR 431.8mm (17in)
Frame: steel rectangular box
Suspension: front, 40mm (1.57in) diameter Marzocchi USD fork; rear, cantilever swing arm
Fuel tank: 22 litres (4.84Imp gal / 5.81US gal)
Measurements: overall length 2150mm (84.65in); width 785mm (30.91in); height 1210mm (47.64in); wheelbase 1490mm (58.66in); seat height 800mm (31.50in)
Dry weight: 226kg (498lb)

MOTO GUZZI

Above: the Le Mans is the first bike in the 1100 V series to use a half-fairing. The Le Mans Tenni (**inset**) is named after the great Omobono Tenni, who gained his first race victory in 1924 while still a teenager and rode for Moto Guzzi from 1933, winning on all of the Italian circuits as well as winning the Tourist Trophy

125

MV AGUSTA

In July 2001 the famous MV marque was reborn as MV Agusta Motorcycles SpA, thanks to the intervention of Piaggio which took a twenty percent holding in the company. Production is still centered on Schiranna, but owing to expansion it has renovated the factories at Morazzone and Cassinetta, the three sites handling respectively the production of engines, frames and final assembly.

The MV models for 2002 included the F4 range with the S, S 1+1, Senna (a limited edition dedicated to the racing driver Ayrton Senna), and the SPR, as well as the Brutale models.

Below: *the 2002 Brutale Oro model uses the same engine as the F4 S **below right**, with the same bore and stroke but with the output adjusted to 93kW (125.6hp) at 12,500rpm. These two models also have the same specification for the wheels and tyres, although the Brutale is slightly larger throughout all major dimensions. However, it has a slightly smaller fuel tank, a tubular steel trellis frame and an electronically-limited maximum speed of 250km/h (155.3mph)*

MV AGUSTA

F4 S

Engine type: liquid-cooled, with water-oil heat exchanger, four-cylinder, four-stroke, with four valves per cylinder
Bore x stroke: 73.8 x 43.8mm (2.91 x 1.72in)
Displacement: 749.4cc
Compression ratio: 12:1
Output: 100.7kW (136bhp) at 12,600rpm
Transmission: six-speed
Brakes: front, double steel 310mm (12.2in) diameter floating disc; rear, 210mm (8.27in) diameter single steel disc
Tyres: front, 120 / 65 ZR 431.8mm (17in) 56W; rear, 190 / 50 ZR 431.8mm (17in) 73W or 180 / 55 ZR 431.8mm (17in) 73W
Suspension: front, upside-down telescopic hydraulic fork; rear, progressive single shock absorber
Fuel tank: 21 litres (4.62Imp gal / 5.54US gal)
Measurements: overall length 2007mm (79.01in); width 685mm (26.97in); wheelbase 1398mm (55.04in); seat height 790mm (31.10in)
Dry weight: 191kg (421.1lb)
Maximum speed: 283km/h (175.7mph)

ROYAL ENFIELD

Royal-Enfield was established at Redditch, England, in 1898, and at first made three-wheelers with De Dion engines, then motorcycles with 211cc Minerva engines mounted above the front wheel. During the 1930s the range included the now famous Bullet models, with 248cc, 346cc and 499cc ohv single-cylinder engines.

In 1955 a trading association with Madras Motors in India was established to help meet demand from the Indian Army, and when the Redditch factory closed in 1970, the Indian company, then called Enfield India Ltd, continued to make the Bullet models which had first appeared in their current form in 1949.

In 1994 Enfield India Ltd was acquired by the Eicher Engineering Group which set up a new plant at Jaipur (Rajasthan) in 1999, where it produces both 350cc and 500cc Bullet models in both classic and deluxe versions. Other models include the 500-S Clubman and the trials-styled 350-T.

Below: *the 2001 version of the Bullet 350DL model*

ROYAL ENFIELD

Above: Enfield's 500 Clubman GT is another of the models now available that evoke nostalgic memories of a famous marque that has been exported all around the world, both from England and from India

BULLET 350

Engine type: four-stroke, ohv single-cylinder
Bore x stroke: 70 x 90mm (2.76 x 3.54in)
Displacement: 346cc
Compression ratio: 5.5:1
Output: 14.8kW (20bhp)
Transmission: four-speed
Fuel tank: 14.5 litres (3.19Imp gal / 3.83US gal)
Measurements: wheelbase 1370mm (53.9in); seat height 775mm (30.5in)
Dry weight: 159kg (351lb)

BULLET 500

Engine type: four-stroke, ohv single-cylinder
Bore x stroke: 84 X 90mm (3.31 x 3.54in)
Displacement: 499cc
Compression ratio: 5.5:1
Output: 17.4kW (24bhp)
Transmission: four-speed
Fuel tank: 20 litres (4.40Imp gal / 5.29US gal)
Measurements: wheelbase 1370mm (53.9in); seat height 775mm (30.5in)
Dry weight: 161kg (355lb)

129

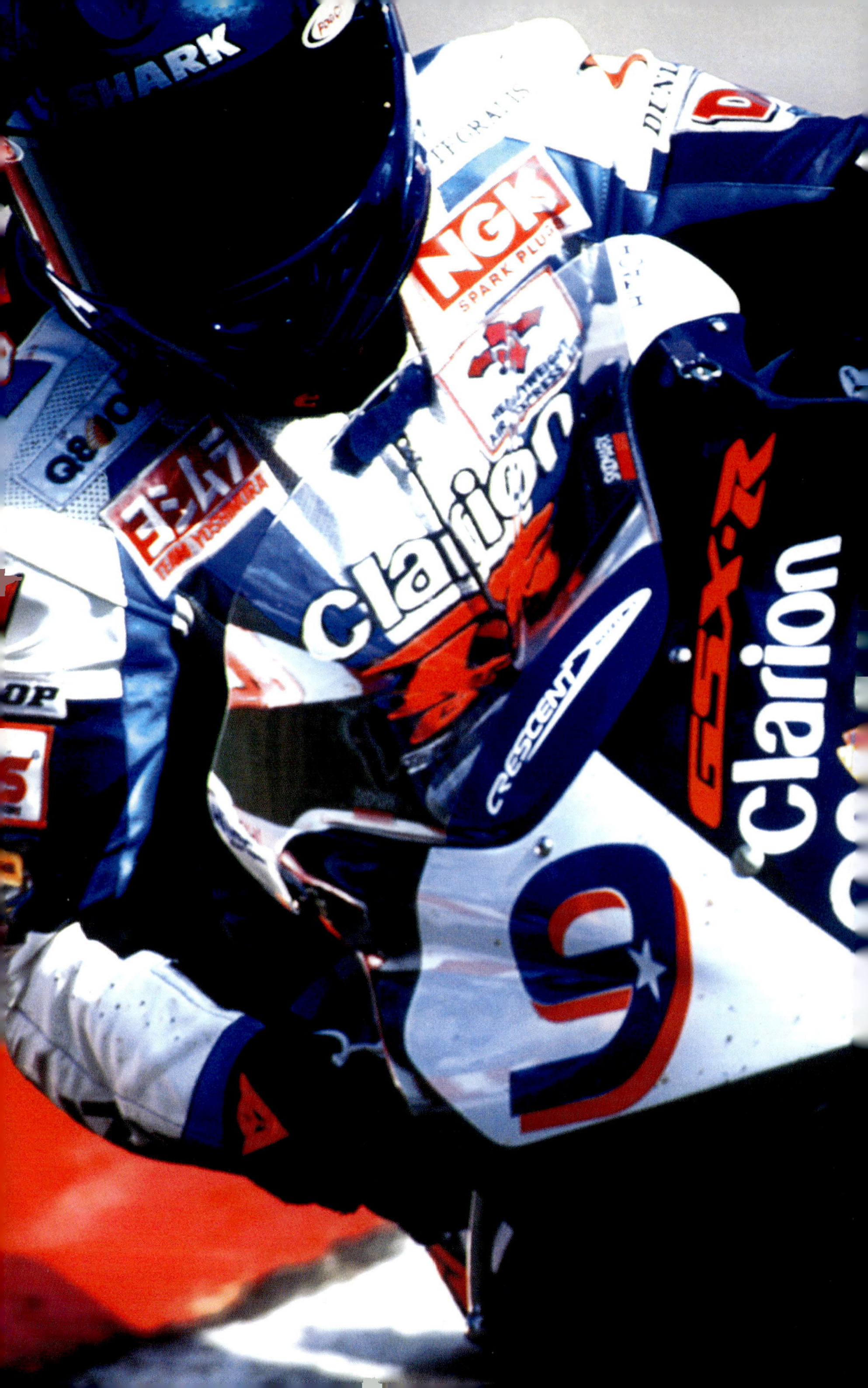
SHARK
NGK
SPARK PLUG
clarion
GSX-R
Clarion
CRESCENT
9

SUZUKI

Left: *Clarion Suzuki GSX-R Factory Squad star Karl Harris totally dominated the second half of the 2001 British Supersport Championship season on his GSX-R600*

SUZUKI

The Suzuki Motor Co. Ltd was formed in Takatsuka, Japan, in 1936, but its first bike did not appear until 1951. It soon gained a reputation for excellent two-strokes that in the early years were mostly small-capacity bikes like the 49cc mokicks.

Suzuki two-strokes were winning many of the big European races from the 1960s onwards, including TT races with 49cc water-cooled machines and 124cc models. In the 1970s a Suzuki won the World 500cc Championship with the late Barry Sheene in the saddle, and at the same time the company was also winning World Moto-cross Championships.

In 1978 Suzuki launched the landmark GS1000, a well-mannered open-class superbike, and a direct challenger to Kawasaki's Z1. It was powered by a 997cc engine that used twin cams and eight valves to produce 87bhp and a top speed of 216km/h (135mph). The company pioneered the dual-sport market in the early 1990s with the introduction of the legendary DR350, and at the end of the century the all-new DR-Z400. The new millennium saw Suzuki's GSX-R1000 race replica bike named as *MCN* Machine of the Year, *Superbike* SuperBike of the Year, and *Performance Bikes* Sportsbike of the Year, while on the track the works rider Karl Harris won the British Supersports Championship on a GSX-R600, and privateer Paul Young took the British Superstock Championship on a GSX-R1000.

In 2002 Suzuki launched three new models which are included here, together with some of the more familiar favorites such as the Bandit, Custom, Commuter and Dual Purpose machines. Its comprehensive range includes superbikes, ultimate sports, V-twin sports, naked sports and sports tourers, and now, with the introduction of the V-Strom, also adventure sports.

Right: *Suzuki's Supersports bikes are the GSX-R1000 (illustrated), GSX-R750 and the GSX-R600. The R1000, named the Machine of the Year in 2001, took the following championships that year: the British Superstock, Australian Superbike, European Superstock and the Super Production World Cup-Endurance Championship, while its sister bikes took the British Superbike Privateers Cup and the American AMA Superbike Championship (both by the R750) and the British Supersport and the Australian Supersport Championships (by the R600)*

The GSX-R750, on which the other two bikes are based, was launched in 1985 and is believed to have won more races than any other motorcycle

GSX-R1000

Engine type: liquid-cooled, four-stroke, dohc four-cylinder
Bore x stroke: 73 x 59mm (2.87 x 2.32in)
Displacement: 988cc
Compression ratio: 12.0:1
Starter: electric
Transmission: six-speed
Brakes: front, 6-piston callipers, dual disc; rear, 2-piston calliper disc
Tyres: front, 120 / 70 ZR 431.8mm (17in); rear, 190 / 50 ZR 431.8mm (17in)
Suspension: front, titanium nitrate coated inverted telescopic tubes, coil spring, spring preload fully adjustable, rebound and compression damping force fully adjustable; rear, link type, oil damped, coil spring, spring preload fully adjustable
Fuel tank: 18 litres (3.96Imp gal / 4.76US gal)
Measurements: overall length 2045mm (80.5in); width 715mm (28.1in); height 1135mm (44.6in); wheelbase 1410mm (55.5in); seat height 830mm (32.3in); ground clearance 130mm (5.1in)
Dry weight: 170kg (375lb)

GSX1300R HAYABUSA

Engine type: liquid-cooled, four-stroke, dohc in-line four-cylinder with four valves per cylinder
Bore x stroke: 81 x 63mm (3.19 x 2.48in)
Displacement: 1,298cc
Compression ratio: 11.0:1
Starter: electric
Transmission: six-speed
Brakes: front, 6-piston callipers, 320mm (12.60in) diameter dual floating discs; rear, opposed 2-piston calliper, 240mm (9.45in) diameter disc
Tyres: front, 120 / 70 ZR 431.8mm (17in); rear, 190 / 50 ZR 431.8mm (17in)
Suspension: front, 43mm (1.69in) diameter inverted telescopic fork, coil spring, oil damped, fully adjustable spring preload; rear, swing arm type with progressive linkage, five-way adjustable spring preload
Fuel tank: 22 litres (4.84Imp gal / 5.81US gal)
Measurements: overall length 2140mm (84.3in); width 740mm (29.1in); height 1155mm (45.5in); wheelbase 1485mm (58.5in); seat height 805mm (31.7in); ground clearance 120mm (4.7in)
Dry weight: 215kg (474lb)

Below: Suzuki's ultimate sports bike, with the lowest drag co-efficient of any of its street motorcycles

SUZUKI

SV650

Engine type: liquid-cooled, four-stroke, dohc two-cylinder 90 degree V-twin with four valves per cylinder
Bore x stroke: 81 x 62.6mm (3.19 x 2.46in)
Displacement: 645cc
Compression ratio: 11.5:1
Starter: electric
Transmission: six-speed
Brakes: front, 290mm (11.42in) diameter dual discs; two-piston calliper; rear, 240mm (9.45in) diameter disc, two-piston calliper
Tyres: front, 120 / 60 ZR 431.8mm (17in); rear, 160 / 60 ZR 431.8mm (17in)
Suspension: front, 41mm (1.61in) diameter telescopic fork, coil spring, gas / oil damped; rear, link type, coil spring, gas / oil damped, seven-way adjustable spring preload
Fuel tank: 16 litres (3.52Imp gal / 4.23US gal)
Measurements: overall length 2070mm (81.5in); width 750mm (29.5in); height 1060mm (41.7in); wheelbase 1430mm (56.3in); seat height 805mm (31.7in); ground clearance 140mm (5.5in)
Dry weight: 165kg (636lb)

Above: the V-twin is also available semi-faired (SV650S)

GSX1400

Engine type: air / oil-cooled, four-stroke, dohc four-cylinder
Bore x stroke: 81 x 68mm (3.19 x 2.68in)
Displacement: 1,402cc
Compression ratio: 9.5:1
Starter: electric
Transmission: six-speed
Brakes: front, 6-piston callipers, dual discs; rear, 2-piston calliper, disc
Tyres: front, 120 / 70 ZR 431.8mm (17in); rear, 190 / 50 ZR 431.8mm (17in)
Suspension: front, telescopic, coil spring, inner cartridge, spring preload adjustable, rebound and compression damping force 12-way adjustable; rear, swing arm type, oil damped, coil spring, spring pre-load hydraulically adjustable, rebound and compression damping force four-way adjustable
Fuel tank: 22 litres (4.84Imp gal / 5.81US gal)
Measurements: overall length 2160mm (85.0in); width 810mm (31.9in); height 1140mm (44.9in); wheelbase 1520mm (59.8in); seat height 790mm (31.1in); ground clearance 130mm (5.1in)
Dry weight: 228kg (502lb)

Below: Suzuki's naked sport GSX1400, which was introduced in 2001

GSX600F

Engine type: air-cooled with SACS, four-stroke, dohc in-line four-cylinder with four valves per cylinder
Bore x stroke: 62.6 x 48.7mm (2.46 x 1.92in)
Displacement: 600cc
Compression ratio: 11.3:1
Starter: electric
Transmission: six-speed
Brakes: front, two-piston callipers, 290mm (11.42in) diameter dual discs; rear, two-piston calliper, 240mm (9.45in) diameter disc
Tyres: front, 120 / 70 ZR 431.8mm (17in); rear, 150 / 70 ZR 431.8mm (17in)
Suspension: front, 41mm (1.61in) diameter telescopic fork, coil spring, oil damped, four-way adjustable rebound damping; rear, link type with progressive linkage, coil spring, oil damped, four-step rebound damping, seven-way adjustable spring preload
Fuel tank: 20 litres (4.40Imp gal / 5.29US gal)
Measurements: overall length 2135mm (84.1in); width 745mm (29.3in); height 1195mm (47.0in); wheelbase 1470mm (57.9in); seat height 785mm (30.9in); ground clearance 120mm (4.7in)
Dry weight: 208kg (458lb)

BANDIT

Engine type: air-cooled with SACS, four-stroke, dohc four-cylinder
Bore x stroke: 79 x 59mm (3.11 x 2.32in)
Displacement: 1,157cc
Compression ratio: 9.5:1
Starter: electric
Transmission: five-speed
Brakes: front, dual discs; rear, disc
Tyres: front, 120 / 70 ZR 431.8mm (17in); rear, 180 / 55 ZR 431.8mm (17in)
Fuel tank: 20 litres (4.40Imp gal / 5.29US gal)
Measurements: overall length 2140mm (84.3in); width 765mm (30.1in); height 1100mm (43.3in); wheelbase 1430mm (56.3in); seat height 790mm (31.1in); ground clearance 130mm (5.1in)
Dry weight: 214kg (471lb)

Above: the naked Bandit GSF1200 is also available half-faired, and with a smaller capacity 600cc engine

CUSTOM

Engine type: air-cooled, four-stroke, sohc 45 degree V-twin with three valves per cylinder
Bore x stroke: 96 x 101mm (3.78 x 3.98in)
Displacement: 1,462cc
Compression ratio: 8.5:1
Starter: electric
Transmission: five-speed
Brakes: front, 300mm (11.81in) disc; rear, 275mm (10.82in) disc
Tyres: front, 150 / 80 406mm (16in); rear, 180 / 70 381mm (15in)
Fuel tank: 15.5 litres (3.41Imp gal / 4.10US gal)
Measurements: overall length 2525mm (99.4in); width 965mm (38.0in); height 1165mm (45.9in); wheelbase 1700mm (66.9in); seat height 700mm (27.6in); ground clearance 145mm (5.7in)
Dry weight: 296kg (652lb)

Above: the VL1500LC Intruder

SUZUKI

COMMUTER

Engine type: air-cooled, four-stroke, dohc two cylinder
Bore x stroke: 74 x 56.6mm (2.91 x 2.23in)
Displacement: 487cc
Compression ratio: 9.0:1
Starter: electric
Transmission: six-speed
Tyres: front, 110 / 70 279mm (11in) 54H; rear, 130 / 70 431mm (17in) 62H
Fuel tank: 20 litres (4.40Imp gal / 5.29US gal)
Measurements: overall length 2080mm (81.9in); width 820mm (32.3in); height 1080mm (42.5in); wheelbase 1405mm (55.3in); seat height 790mm (31.1in); ground clearance 150mm (5.9in)
Dry weight: 173kg (381lb)

Above: there is just one model in the Suzuki commuter range, the GS500; a sleek-styled sporty bike with a classic parallel twin engine

DUAL PURPOSE

Engine type: liquid-cooled, four-stroke, dohc single-cylinder
Bore x stroke: 90 x 62.6mm (3.54 x 2.46in)
Displacement: 398cc
Compression ratio: 11.3:1
Starter: electric
Transmission: five-speed
Brakes: front, 250mm (9.84in) disc; rear, 220mm (8.66in) disc
Tyres: front, 80 / 100 533mm (21in); rear, 120 / 90 457mm (18in)
Fuel tank: 9.5 litres (2.09Imp gal / 2.51US gal)
Measurements: overall length 2310mm (90.9in); width 875mm (34.4in); height 1240mm (48.8in); wheelbase 1485mm (58.4in); seat height 935mm (36.8in); ground clearance 300mm (11.8in)
Dry weight: 132kg (291lb)

This range includes the DR-Z400S; above, the TS50 and the Freewind

TRIUMPH

The new Triumph bikes were announced at the Köln Show in 1990, with the first production machine, the 4-cylinder 1200cc Trophy, being available in the following year. Since then the reborn company has established a reputation for producing a high quality, reliable, and well-engineered machines with that very distinctive British character.

The Daytona T955 and the T509 Speed Triple were both launched in 1996, and are still present in a current range that also includes the Sprint RS and ST, the Tiger, the TT600 and the Bonneville.

Below: *the awesome Daytona 955i, which was heavily revised in 2001, is now sharper, lighter and faster than ever, and remains the flagship of the Triumph range. Powered by Triumph's second-generation fuel-injected engine (a liquid-cooled dohc in-line 3-cylinder of 955cc capacity), the Daytona breathes easier, runs cooler and revs higher, and packs a mighty 109kW (147bhp) punch*

BONNEVILLE AMERICA

Engine type: air-cooled, dohc, parallel twin
Bore x stroke: 86 x 68mm (3.89 x 2.68in)
Displacement: 790cc
Compression ratio: 9.2:1
Output: 45kW (61bhp) at 7,400 rpm
Transmission: five-speed
Brakes: front, single 310mm (12.20in) disc, 2 piston calliper; rear, single 285mm 11.22in) disc, 2 piston calliper
Tyres: front, 110 / 80 R 457.2mm (18in); rear, 170 / 80 R 381mm (15in)
Frame: tubular steel cradle swing arm
Suspension: front, 41mm (1.61in) forks; rear, chromed spring twin shocks with adjustable pre-load
Fuel tank: 16.6 litres (3.65Imp gal / 4.4 US gal)
Measurements: overall length 2424mm (95.4in); width (handlebars) 955mm (37.6in); height 1184mm (46.6in); wheelbase 1655mm (65.2in); seat height 720mm (28.3in)
Dry weight: 226kg (497lb)

MODERN MOTORCYCLES

Left: the Trophy 1200
Right: Triumph's street fighter, the Speed Triple

TRIUMPH

Top left: the Sprint ST which is a superb sports tourer is also available as the half-faired RS
Above: the TT600
Right: the Tiger

YAMAHA

The second generation YZF-R1 supersport (*illustrated below*) is just one of five current new Yamaha motorcycles. Improved beyond all recognition, it now boasts an all-new fuel injection system that provides instant throttle response as well as improved fuel efficiency and reduced emissions from the awesomely quick 998cc in-line four-cylinder engine.

The YZF-R1 joins the 599cc R6 in the flagship category, while in the sports touring category there is a new entrant in the form of the TDM900, and the street bike line-up was enhanced with the unveiling of the FZS600 Fazer. There is yet more muscle, in the shape of the XJR1300 and the robust BT1100 Bulldog V-twin.

Yamaha has not made any further additions to its Adventure Sport range, the 125cc or Cruiser ranges, but its strength in these areas remains undiminished.

TDM900

Engine type: liquid-cooled, dohc, four-stroke, twin with five valves per cylinder
Displacement: 897cc
Output: 63.4kW (82.2bhp) at 7,500rpm
Transmission: six-speed
Brakes: front, dual disc; rear, single disc
Tyres: front, 120 / 70 ZR 457.2mm (18in) M/C 59W; rear, 160 / 60 ZR 431.8mm (17in) M/C 69W
Frame: all-new lightweight aluminium with swing arm
Suspension: front, telescopic forks; rear, link suspension
Fuel tank: 20 litres (4.40Imp gal / 5.29 US gal)
Measurements: overall length 2180mm (85.83in); width 800mm (31.50in); height 1290mm (50.79in); wheelbase 1485mm (58.46in)
Dry weight: 190kg (419lb)

XJR1300

Engine type: air-cooled, dohc, four-stroke, four-cylinder with 16 valves
Displacement: 1251cc
Output: 78.1kW (106.2bhp) at 8,000rpm
Transmission: five-speed
Brakes: front, dual disc; rear, single disc
Tyres: front, 120 / 70 ZR 431.8mm (17in) 58W; rear, 180 / 55 ZR 431.8mm (17in) 73W
Frame: high rigidity double-cradle
Suspension: front, telescopic forks; rear, dual shock
Fuel tank: 21 litres (4.62Imp gal / 5.55 US gal)
Measurements: overall length 2175mm (85.63in); width 775mm (30.51in); height 1115mm (43.90in); wheelbase 1510mm (59.45in)
Dry weight: 224kg (494lb)

BT1100 BULLDOG

Engine type: air-cooled, sohc, four-stroke, V-twin
Displacement: 1063cc
Output: 47.8kW (65bhp) at 5,500 rpm
Transmission: five-speed
Brakes: front, dual floating disc; rear, single disc
Tyres: front, 120 / 70 ZR 431.8mm (17in); rear, 170 / 60 ZR 431.8mm (17in)
Frame: steel twin backbone
Suspension: front, telescopic forks; rear, swing arm
Fuel tank: 20 litres (4.40Imp gal / 5.29 US gal)
Measurements: overall length 2200mm (86.61in); width 800mm (31.50in); height 1140mm (44.88in); wheelbase 1530mm (60.24in)
Dry weight: 229kg (505lb)

MODERN MOTORCYCLES

FZS600 FAZER

Engine type: liquid-cooled, dohc, four-stroke, in-line four-cylinder with 16 valves
Displacement: 599cc
Output: 69.9kW (95bhp) at 11,500rpm
Transmission: six-speed
Brakes: front, dual 298mm (11.73in) floating disc; rear, single disc
Tyres: front, 110 / 70 ZR 431.8mm (17in) 54W; rear, 160 / 60 ZR 431.8mm (17in) 69W
Frame: highly rigid double cradle
Suspension: front, telescopic forks with adjustable preload; rear, link suspension
Fuel tank: 22 litres (4.84Imp gal / 5.81 US gal)
Measurements: overall length 2080mm (81.89in); width 710mm (27.95in); height 1180mm (46.46in); wheelbase 1415mm (55.71in)
Dry weight: 189kg (417lb)

YAMAHA

GLOSSARY

A

advanced ignition: describes the setting of the ignition timing of the engine so that the spark occurs at the plug points before the piston reaches the top of the stroke
air cooling: a method of dispersing the heat that is produced by the engine's cylinders
air intake: the port through which the air supply to the carburettor is drawn
atmospheric inlet valve: common on early machines, this valve is opened by the vacuum in the cylinder created by the falling piston
automatic inlet valves: used on early engines, they opened without any mechanical control

B

ball joint: a ball at the end of a rod or lever rotates in a socket of another member
bellmouth: an air intake trumpet which is attached to the carburettor
belt-drive: often made from leather, belts transmitted power from the engine or gearbox to the rear wheel
bevel drive: usually refers to gear which actuates the overhead camshaft; also sometimes used in shaft-drive systems, or to actuate magnetos

bhp (brake horse power): a measurement of the engine's maximum power output available at the engine flywheel
bialbero *see* **dohc**
big end: the lower part of the connecting rod at the point where it is attached to the crank pin
bore: the measurement of the diameter of a cylinder
bottom dead centre: describes the position of the piston when it reaches the lowest point in its travel within the cylinder, and is about to begin its upward journey

C

cam: rotating eccentric used to control valve or ignition timing, also used to operate drum brakes
camshaft: the shaft or spindle, with or upon which the cam rotates
capacity: the capacity of engine cylinders is expressed in cubic centimetres (cc) in Europe
carburettor: the device in which fuel and air are mixed into a combustible vapour
Cardan shaft: used as a drive, instead of the chain, from the gearbox to the rear wheel
chain drive: the transmission of power from one sprocket-wheel to another by means of a chain. Mostly used for driving the rear wheel,

GLOSSARY

although also used for transmitting the power from engine to gearbox, magneto or overhead camshaft
chair: a sidecar
charge: the volume of fuel vapour and air which is sucked into the cylinder by the induction stroke of the piston
clincher rims: a rim that was used with some early inflatable tyres
clip-ons: sports or racing handlebars that are positioned low onto the front forks by clamps
combination: a motorcycle fitted with a sidecar
combustion chamber: the space in the cylinder above the piston where the explosive charge is compressed and ignited
connecting rod: a light metal bar which connects the underside of the piston to the crankshaft
contact breaker: a mechanical switch which constantly breaks and restores a low-tension ignition circuit to create ignition from the spark plug
cradle: a motorcycle frame in which the engine is sited between two frame tubes
crankcase: the metal casing surrounding the crankshaft and its assembly
crankpin: the shorter part of the crankshaft, it receives the downward thrust of the piston
crankshaft: the vital revolving shaft of the engine, it converts the linear movement of the piston into rotational movement
constant loss: a system of lubrication or ignition that does not have a circuit for the oil or electricity to return to the oil tank or the battery
cylinder: the cylindrical metal chamber in which the combustion of the fuel takes place, thereby converting the fuel into power

D

dohc: double overhead camshafts
distributor: a device in the ignition system of some multi-cylinder engines that sends the high-tension spark to the correct cylinder
dry-sump lubrication: an engine lubrication system in which two oil-pumps are used. One feeds oil from the reservoir around the engine bearings under pressure, the other removes the surplus oil from the sump and returns it to the oil reservoir

E

exhaust: the pipe through which the exhaust gases from the cylinder are expelled into the air
exhaust gases: the products that result from the combustion taking place in the cylinders. They normally consist of carbon dioxide, carbon monoxide, nitrogen and steam plus a varying amount of oil-vapour, unburnt fuel and hydrocarbon gases
exhaust stroke: the upward stroke of the piston. The action pushes out the burnt charge within the cylinder through the raised exhaust valve

GLOSSARY

exhaust valve: the cylinder valve of the engine which permits the escape of the combustion mixture. It is opened once per two revolutions of the flywheel

F

fairing: an enclosure over the front of the bike used to improve either the machines aerodynamics or the rider's comfort
fins: the thin metal ribs outside air-cooled cylinders so designed as to present as great a surface as possible to the cooling action of the air
flat: an engine in which the cylinders are placed at 180 degrees to each other; a horizontal engine
float: part of the carburettor which regulates the supply of petrol to the float bowl
float bowl/chamber: a metal case or cylinder acting as the carburettor fuel reservoir, into which the flow of the fuel is controlled by a valve operated by a float
flywheel: used to balance the intermittent power impulses supplied to the crankshaft by the pistons, and thus permit the steady running of the engine, this wheel of heavy steel or cast-iron is mounted on the main shaft of the engine
four-stroke cycle: the engine cycle which has four basic operations, or piston movements – induction, compression, combustion and exhaust

friction drive: an older form of friction gear having a series of friction discs which make variable contact with the flywheel from which the drive is taken, rather than the usual gearbox-clutch assembly

G

gasket: a washer made from a variety of packing materials, placed between two metal faces in order to produce a gas-tight joint
gate change: an old method of changing gears with a hand lever, by moving the gear-lever into various positions in the gate
gearbox: comprised of a train of pinion wheels arranged in a metal casing; various combinations of the wheels can be engaged, thereby enabling the power generated by the engine to be transmitted via the crankshaft to the road-wheels in varying ratios
gear ratio: the ratio between the input and the output speeds of a train of gear wheels, and expressed as the ratio of engine revolutions to the number of road-wheel revolutions
girder forks: an early form of front suspension in which the front wheel is held in a set of forks which are attached to the steering head by parallel links
gudgeon pin: a thin steel rod which enables power to be transmitted to the crankshaft; it passes horizontally through the underside of the piston,

and serves to connect the small end of the connecting rod to the piston

H

horizontally opposed engine *see* **flat**
horsepower: the power required to raise 33,000lb by 1 foot in 1 minute (in metric terms 14,982kg by 30.48cm in one minute)

I

ignition timing: usually expressed in degrees, it is the position of the crankshaft when the spark occurs relative to 0 degrees

indicated horsepower: the amount of power that is expended by the burning of the fuel mixture in driving the piston downwards, but because this measurement does not account for the amount of power lost by friction within the engine it does not represent the external power output of the engine

induction pipe: a conduit which conveys the explosive mixture from the carburettor to the engine cylinders

inlet manifold: a tube which connects the carburettor to the inlet port

inlet over exhaust (ioe): a valve layout in which the inlet valve is placed directly above the exhaust valve

inlet valve: operated by means of a cam, the valve admits the mixture of fuel vapour and air into the cylinder at regular intervals

L

leading-link: a front suspension arrangement in which a short link pivots at the foot of a solid fork. A spring controls the movement of the axle which is mounted on the front of the link

leading shoe: the first of two shoes which engage the rotating drum when breaking

leaf springs: springs that are compiled from a number of layers of spring steel leaves which are clamped together. A method that was originally used on rear suspension and front forks, but obsolete since the 1930s

little end: the upper end and bearing of the connecting-rod at its point of connection to the gudgeon-pin of the piston

M

magneto: a dynamo which is comprised of an armature which revolves between the poles of one or more permanent magnets. It is used as a generator of high-tension current for ignition purposes

manifold: a short passage or a chamber through which gases may flow; for example, an exhaust manifold is one through which the gases flow from the exhaust ports of

GLOSSARY

the cylinders. Also used to refer to the induction pipe assembly
megaphone: a tapered performance exhaust

O

ohc: overhead camshaft
open cradle: a frame designed without any lower frame tubes, but that utilises the engine which is bolted into place to form part of the frame as a stressed member
outfit *see* **sidecar**
overhead valve (ohv): valves positioned above the combustion chamber and opened by pushrods from a low camshaft

P

plunger: (a) a rear suspension system with the axle mounted between two vertical springs; (b) a small piston with a hand-operating stem and knob, used as a forcer of liquids in small pumps, including suspension units
poppet valve: an ordinary type of valve found in four-stroke engines
port: a passage or opening leading to the interior of the cylinder, through which gases are drawn or expelled
port timing: in a two-stroke engine, the moment when the ports are masked or unmasked
pre-unit: on older machines, where the engine and gearbox were constructed as separate parts
primary drive: the unit which transfers the power from the engine to the clutch/gearbox
pushrods: in ohv engines, the rods used to transmit the lift of the camshaft lobes to the tappets

R

retarded ignition: ignition timing of the engine set so that the spark occurs at the plug points after the piston has reached the top of its stroke, and has thus begun its downward journey
rocker: a pivoted lever that conveys movement from one point to another in valve mechanisms
rotary valve: normally mounted in the side-valve position, it is driven off the camshaft by means of a spiral screw to provide successive communication between the cylinder and the exhaust pipe

S

side-valve: the position of the valves in relation to the cylinder
silencer: a device fitted to the exhaust system to reduce the pressure of the exhaust gases before they reach the outside air
slide valve: an engine valve in which the entry and exit of the cylinder gases is controlled by two concentric sliding sleeves situated between the piston and the cylinder
snail cam chain adjusters: helical-shaped cams on the axle that allow the chain to be adjusted accurately
sohc: single overhead camshaft
spine: a type of frame where the

GLOSSARY

main structure which connects the steering head and swing arm pivot has the engine suspended beneath it
stressed member: usually refers to the engine, but any component that forms part of the whole frame or structure
stroke: the measurement of the piston's travel during its upward, or downward, movement in the cylinder
suction stroke: the downward stroke of the piston which draws the mixture of fuel vapour and air into the cylinder through the inlet valve
supercharger: a device used to compress the engine's incoming charge so that more fuel vapour and air are taken into the cylinder than would normally occur by the induction stroke of the piston

T

tappet: a steel rod which transmits the lifting motion of the valve cams to the valves so that they are opened regularly
tappet clearance: the tiny space necessary between the end of the valve stem and its tappet in order to accommodate the expansion of the valve stem when heated
throttle: valve which controls the entry of the gaseous mixture into the cylinder(s)
timing: the measurement of the position of the valves, piston or crankshaft relative to the stroke of the piston or revolution of the crankshaft

top dead centre (tdc): the point when the crankshaft and piston are uppermost in their travel, that is, at 0 degrees
trailing link: a front suspension arrangement in which the link pivots at the front of a solid fork, with the axle mounted at the rear
transmission shaft: transmits the power from the gearbox to the rear wheel
twinport: a cylinder head designed with two ports which branch away from a single valve
two-stroke: describes an engine cycle in which the power impulse on the piston occurs at every alternate stroke

U

unit construction: where the engine and gearbox are built within the same casing
universal joint: positioned between two rotating shafts, the joint permits the side-to-side movement of one shaft without severing the power connection between them

V

V-twin: an engine layout that has the cylinders set opposite one another in a letter V formation

W

wheelbase: the distance between the centres of the front and rear wheels

INDEX

General Index

American Dirt Track Championship 64
Auriol, Hubert 65, **65**
Bayliss, Troy 98
Biaggi, Max 75
Bloor, John 66
Bosch, Robert 14
Bouton, Georges 12
Buell, Erik 66
Daimler Gottlieb, 9, **10**, 11, 12
Daimler, Paul 12
Davidson, Douglas 40
de Dion, Comte Albert 12
De Tomaso, Alejandro 66
Drew, Alfred 15
Dunlop, John Boyd 12, 81
Dunlop Rubber Company 81
Edwards, Colin 108
First World War 18, 33, 46
Fogarty, Karl 29
Ford, Model T 18
Gardener, Wayne 68, **69**
Grand Prix, Ulster 46
Handstrom, Oscar 16
Harris, Karl, 131 132
Hendee, George 16
Henderson, W 44
Hildebrand, Heinrich 12
Hildebrand, Wilhelm 12
Honda, Soichiro 25
Jaguar Car Co 40
Karrer, Philipp 40
Köln Show 140
Lemon, Arthur 44
Lyons, William 40
Maybach, Wilhelm 9, 12
Otto, Dr Nikolaus 79
Parker, Scott 64, **64**
Pitt, Andrew 114, **114**
Rahier, Gaston 65, **65**
Rally, Paris-Dakar 65, 120
Reutlingen Brotherhood 12
Scrambling Championship, European 55
Second World War 20, 21, 46, 54, 57, 61, 80
Senna, Ayrton 126
Service School, Harley-Davidson **38**, 39
Sheene, Barry 132
Starch, Philippe 75
Superbike Championship
  American AMA 132
  Australian 132
  British, Privateers Cup 132
  World 98, 108
Supersport Championship
  Australian 132
  British 131, 132
  FIM World 600, 114
Superstock Championship
  British 132
  European 132
Tenni, Omobono 125
Tourist Trophy (TT)
  Clubman's 52
  Isle of Man 25, 54, 108, 125, 132
Trial, Scottish Six Days 55
  World Championship 61
von Opel, Fritz 40
Walker, Otto 40, **41**
Walmsley, William 40
Wankel, Felix 79
Werner, Eugene 14
Werner, Michel 14
Willis, Harold 19
Wolfmüller, Alois 12
World Championship
  125cc 84
  250cc 75, 84
  500cc 68, 108, 132
  Moto-cross 120, 132
World Cup Endurance
  Championship, Super Production 132
Young, Paul 132

Based on 1962 Los Angeles Police Department 1,200cc Model FL Harley-Davidsons, Peter Fonda's Easy Rider Chopper for the 1969 film was stolen. This 1993 replica is on view at the Otis Chandler Vintage Museum of Transportation and Wildlife, Oxnard, Ca

INDEX

Motorcycles and Manufacturers

ACE 16
AJS 21, 24, 50
Aprilia 78, 84, 122
   Caponord ETV 1000 84, 86, **86**
   Falco R SL 1000 84, **84**, 85
   Futura RST 1000 84, 86, **86**
   Moto' 6.5, **74**, 75???
   Pegaso I E 650 84, 87, **87**
   RS250 **72/73**, 75
   RSV Mille R 1, **2**, **82/83**, 83, 84
   RX 50, 84, 87, **87**
Ariel 25, 46
   NH 21
   Red Hunter 46, **47**
   Square Four 20, **20,** 46
Associated Motor Cycles Ltd 50
Astoria 44
Audi 50
Automoto 25
Auto Union AG 50

B

Bark 45
Beeston 15
Benelli 18, 66
   900 66, **66**
   Sei 66
Bianchi 55
   Sportster 55, **55**
Bimota 68
   Testi 1D, 68, **68**
BMW 18, 20, 30, 33, 65, 79, 88
   F 650 CS 88
   F 650 GS 88
   F 650 GS Dakar 88, **88**
   K 75 C 65, **65**, 75, 79
   K 100 65, **65**
   K 100 RS 65, **65**
   K 100 RT 65, **65**
   K 1200 RS **74**, 75, 88, 89, **89**
   R 32 18, **18**
   R 45 63, **63**
   R 50/5 58
   R 60/5 58
   R 75 22, **22**
   R 75/5 58, **58/59**
   R 80 G/S 64, **64**
   R 90 S 28, **28**, 62, **62**
   R 1100 RS 75
   R 1150 GS 90, **90**
   R 1150 R 88
   R 1150 RS 88, 91, **91**
   R 1150 RT 88
   R 1200 C 88
Brough 20
BSA (British Small Arms) 25, 48, 50, 53, 56, 60
   Bantam 23, 54
   Clubman 54
   Golden Flash 54
   Gold Star 54, **54**
   Hornet 56
   Lightning 56, **57**
   Rocket 26, **27**
   Royal Star 56
   Spitfire 56
   Star 56
   Super Rocket 54
   Thunderbolt 56
   Victor 56
Buell 66, 92
   Cyclone M2, 93, **93**
   Firebolt XB9R 4, **4/5**, **78/79**, 79, 92, 94, **94/95**, 95
   Lightning X1 4, **4/5**, 92, **92**, 93
   RR1000 66
   RS1200 66, **67**
   White Lightning X1W 92

C

Cagiva 96
   Mito **96**, 97
   Navigator **96**, 97
   Planet **96**, 97
   Raptor 97
   V Raptor 97, **97**
Champion 39

D

Daimler Riding Car (*Einspur*)1, **2**, 6, 8, **8/9**, 9, **10/11**, 11
De Dion Bouton et Cie 13, 34, 46, 54, 128
DKW 21, 23, 50
   RT 125, 50, **51**, 57
Douglas 24
   Dragonfly 23, **23**
Ducati 28, 79, 98

INDEX

750GT 62, **62**
750SS 28, 100
900 Super Sport 62, 68, 98, 100, **100**
916 29
998R 98, **98**
Infostrada 98
M900 Monster 29, **29**, 68, **69**, 98
Multistrada 1000 98, 99, **99**
Desmo 62
ST4 Sporttouring 100, 101, **101**
Dunelt 24

E
Eicher Engineering Group 128
  Bullet 128; see also Royal Enfield
Enfield India Ltd 128
  Bullet 128; see also Royal Enfield
Excelsior 16, 24
Express 50

F
Fafnir 33
Fichtel & Sachs 50
FN 25, 34, 37
Francis-Barnett 21, 24

G
Garelli 45
Gilera 102
  DNA 102, **102**, 103
  GP Experience 103
  ICE 102
  Supersport 600 102, 103, **103**
Göricke 33
Greeves 55

H
Harley-Davidson 16, 19, 20, 21, 24, 30, **31,** 33, 34, 37, 40, 48, 64, 66, 75, 79, 92, 104, 106
7D 34, **35**
35 Sport 39, **39**
Duo Glide 75
Dyna Glide 105, **105**
Electra Glide 60, 107, **107**
Forty-five 21
Model U 21, **21**
Softail 106, **106**
Sportster 60, 66, 104, **104**, 105
Super Glide 60
Ultra Classic Electra Glide 75, **75**
V-Rod 1, **3**, 104
WLA 21
Hecker 52
Henderson 37
Hildebrand & Wolfmüller 12, 13, **13**, 15
Hiro 84
Hochland 43
Honda, 24, 26, 29, 61, 78, 104, 108
  A-Type 24, **24**
  CB750 26, 28, 79
  CB900F Hornet 108, 111, **111**
  CBR600F Sport 108
  CBX1000 28, 79
  CRF450R 108, **108**
  Dream CB 750 Four 25, **25**
  Dream D-Type 24, 49, **49**
  Fireblade 108, 110, **110**
  GL1,500 Gold Wing 79
  NS400 78
  NS500 78
  NSR500 68, **69**, 79
  Pan European 108, 112, **112**
  Super Cub C 100 52, **52**
  VFR800Fi 108, 109, **109**
  VTR1000SP-2 108, 113, **113**
Horsch 50
Humber 15
Husqvarna 96

I
Ilo 52
Imperia 45
Indian 16, 19, 20, 21, 24, 43
  ACE 44
  Diamond-Framed Racer 16, **16/17**
  Big Chief 43, **43**
  Chief 43
  Indian-4 44, **44**
  Junior Scout 21
  Powerplus 39, **39**
  Scout 43

J
James 24
  Sports V-Twin 19, **19**
JAP 41, 54
Jawa 43

INDEX

K
Kawasaki 26, 29, 78, 114
  Eliminator 114, 118, **118**
  H1 78
  H2 78
  KX65 114, 115, **115**
  VN1500 Mean Streak 114, 116, **116/117**
  W650 114, 118, **118**
  Z1 26, 27, 62, 132
  Z1300 26
  Z900 62
  Z1000 62, **62**
  ZX-12R Ninja 114, **114**
  ZXR400 119, **119**
  ZZ-R1100 68, **70/71**, 114
  ZZ-R1200 114, 119, **119**
KTM 120, 121
  380 SX, 121, **121**
  950 Rally, **120**, 121
Küchen 44

L
Lambretta 24
Laverda 61
  750 SFC, 61, **61**
Lorenz, 40

M
Madras Motors 128
Martin-Jap 24
Matchless 18, 24, 50, 54
  G3L 21, 54
  G3LS 54
  G50 54 **55**
MCC 34
Minerva 33, 34, 128
Montesa 61
  King Scorpion 61, **61**
Moto Guzzi 18, 19, 28, 68, 79, 122
  1100 Sport 68, 122
  California 68, 122, 123, **123**
  Daytona 1000 68, 122
  Falcone Sport 50, **50**
  Navada 750 68, **68**, 122, **122**
  V11 series 1, **2**, 122, 124, **124/125**, 125
Motosacoche (MAG) 45
MuZ 57

M V Agusta 1, 21, 96, 126
  175CS Competizione 52, **53**
  600 57, **57**
  Brutale 126
  Brutale ORO 126, **126**
  F4 75, **75**, 126
  F4 S 126, 127, **127**
  F4 S 1+1 126
  F4 Senna 126
  F4 SPR 126
MZ (Motorradwerke Zschopau) 50, 57
  Model 250/1 G 57, **57**

N
Nestoria 44
New Hudson 24
New Imperial 20
Norman 24
Norton 20, 21, 60
  Commando 60, **60**
  Dominator 99 52, **52**
  TT **42**, 43
NSU 21, 25, 38
  Moped, 24

O
OEC 24
Opel 40
Orionette 41
Ormonde 15

P
Panther (P&M) 24
Peugeot 17, 18
  Paris-Nice 17, **17**
Pierce 16, 36, 37
Powerful 15
Püch 45
Punch 120

R
Racing Spares 66
  Bonneville 66, **66**
Rotax 120
Royal Enfield 25, 128
  350-T 128
  500-S Clubman 128, 129, **129**
  Bullet 128, **128**, 129
Rudge-Whitworth (Rudge) 19, 20, 46

INDEX

Model Ulster 46, **47**

S

Sachs 52, 84, 120
Scott 18, 19
Singer 15
SM 21
Solex Vélosolex moped 48, **49**
Sturmey-Archer 44
Sunbeam 20, 24, 41, 48
   S7, 48, **49**
   S8, 48
Suzuki 26, 29, 78, 131, 132
   Bandit GSF1200 132, 138, **138**
   Custom VL1500LC Intruder 1, **2**, 132, 138, **138**
   DL1000 V-Strom **80/81**, 81, 132
   DR350 132
   DR-Z400 132, 139, **139**
   Freewind 139
   GS500 Commuter 132, 139, **139**
   GS1000 26, 27, **27**, 132
   GSX600F 137, **137**
   GSX 1300R Hayabusa 134, **134**
   GSX1400 136, **136**
   GSX-R600 **130/131**, 131, 132
   GSX-R750 132
   GSX-R1000 132, 133, **133**
   GT750 78
   R1000 132
   SV650 135, **135**
   TS50 139
Swallow Sidecar Company 40

T

Tandon 24
Triumph 15, 18, 30, 33, 34, 40, 60, 66, 77, 79, 140
   Bonneville 140
   Bonneville America 141, **141**
   Bonneville Special 63, **63**
   Bonneville T120 52, **53**, 61
   Daytona 955i **6/7**, 7, **76/77**, 77
   Daytona T955 140, **140**
   Executive 64, **64**
   Gloria sidecar 40, **40**
   HRW 21
   Model H 38, **38**
   Royal 64
   Speed Triple T509 140, 142, **142/143**
   Speed Twin 57, **57**
   Sprint RS 140, 143
   Sprint ST 140, **142**, 143
   Thunderbird 50, **50**
   Tiger 100 46, **47**, 56, **56**
   Tiger 900 30, **30**
   Tiger T110, 52
   Tiger Trial 64, **64**, 140, 143, **143**
   Trident T150 26, 60, 61, **61**, 77
   Trophy 77, 140, 142, **142**
   TT600 140, 143, **143**
   Twenty-One 57

V

Velocette 18, 24
Vespa 24
Victoria 33, 50
Villiers 24, 55
Vincent 24, 52
   Norvin Special 52, **52**
   Series C Rapide 22, **22**
Vitesse 19

W

Wanderer 43, 50
Werner 14, 15, 33
Wooler, 24

Y

Yamaha 26, 29, 78, 144
   BT1100 Bulldog 144, 147, **147**
   FZS600 Fazer 144, 148, **148/149**
   R6 144
   RD350LC 78
   TDM900 144, 145, **145**
   V-Max 66, **67**
   XJR1300 144, 146, **146**
   YZF-R1 144, **144**

Z

Zedel 33, 38
Zündapp (Zünderland Apparatebau GmbH) 18, 46, 48
   KS600 48, **48**
   KS750 46
Zweirad Union 50